TESTIMONIALS

"Pat Turner's *Skiing Uphill* is a breath of hope for anyone who has ever felt challenged by their life circumstances. Funny, at times terrifying, but never maudlin, we see what is meant by "the power of the human spirit." A courageous story by a courageous woman, both of which readers will find unforgettable."

Paula Coomer, Author

Somebody Should have Scolded the Girl,

and *Jagged Edge of the Sky*

"Pat Turner is an inspiration and a living example that it is possible to find your life's purpose and passion. Her strength in the face of almost unimaginable adversities shows us how to find opportunity in difficult circumstances, move past our perceived limitations, and empower ourselves to take charge of our lives to find success and happiness."

Judi Moreo, Author

You Are More Than Enough: Every Woman's Guide to Purpose, Passion & Power

"Skiing Uphill is a must-read memoir! It reads like a fiction novel filled with emotion, adventure, tragedy, and challenges. You will walk every step of the way with Pat as she meets life 'head-on' with amazing courage and passion. This is a beautifully written story from the first page to the last."

Judy Weaver

Writing Instructor

Retired School Principal

SKIING
UPHILL

By

Pat West Turner

TURNING POINT INTERNATIONAL
LAS VEGAS, NEVADA

Published by Turning Point International

ISBN# 978-0-9968817-4-6
Library of Congress Control Number: 2022918824
First Edition: October, 2022

Layout: Jake Naylor

DEDICATION

Love to my husband, Joe,

for his understanding, off-the-wall humor,

and abundance of patience.

Gratitude to the village

that continually offers love, support, and

encouragement through all my trials and

triumphs.

EPIGRAPH

"The end is also the beginning."

People said this to me as I was about
to graduate high school, but they, nor I,
fully understood how real that statement
was. How could I have known that a few
months before graduation, I would be in
an accident that changed my life forever?
This was not a beginning I asked for and
certainly not one I would wish on anyone
else. But it is what it is! Accept it, learn to
cope with it; deny it, or suffer because of
it...

the choice was up to me.

TABLE OF CONTENTS

Disrupted Expectations   **1**

New Beginnings   **19**

Memories of an

Adventurous Childhood   **25**

Lessons Learnedly   **49**

Dark Memories   **59**

The Challenges of Healing   **71**

Dark and Light Moments   **85**

The Rough Road to Recovery   **101**

First Survive, Then Thrive   **111**

Lessons Learned   **117**

Stretch More   **133**

Small Idea, Big Rewards   **141**

Jokester on a Limb   **161**

Unlikely Encounter   **173**

Freedom on the Mountain   **199**

Discovering New Adventures   **225**

Pushing the Limits   **249**

Gym Rat   **261**

Who Knew? I am Creative!   **275**

ABOUT THE AUTHOR,
PAT WEST TURNER

Pat West Turner lives in East Wenatchee, Washington. with her husband, Joe. She was active at her local ski area, Mission Ridge, where she learned to three-track ski in 1966 and went on to teach others in the years to follow as well as to win The Salem Jaycees' Flying Outriggers race at Hoodoo Bowl as well as the National Amputee Ski Races at Mt. Hood. She later performed with the U. S. Amputee Ski Demonstration team at the 8th Interski in Aspen, Colorado, and competed in the New Zealand NZSTAR Race where she won a Silver Medal.

She received her B.A. in education from Central Washington University and her Fifth Year from the University of Sacramento. Placerville, California was her first teaching assignment, then she finished her career in the Wenatchee area. She enjoys working out at the gym as well as riding a tandem bike with Joe. Her travels include New Zealand, Tahiti, Mexico, and Hawaii. Pat also enjoys watercolor painting, reading, writing, knitting, crocheting, and painting "kindness" rocks. She is known locally as the Bookworm Lady. Her business card reflects her spirit: Goal ~ Educate, Encourage, and Inhabit the World with "Worms" and "Smiles.

FOREWARD

In 1965, Pat Turner, who was 17 years old at the time, was riding in a car that was involved in an accident with a snowplow. The collision was so severe that the damage to Pat's body required the eventual amputation of one of her legs by a team of surgeons led by Dr. Vaughn Smith. As a nurse, I was on a team that cared for her during her recovery. What a privilege that was! She was such a fine young lady, amazing in many ways. My heart was open to being the best nurse possible for Pat because of the traumatic accident she was involved in. I remember when she was admitted. My motherly and nurse instincts surfaced at the same time in sympathy for her and her family. I had pre-teen girls of my own at the time. As I write this, tears come to my eyes because of reliving what that family went through. As time elapsed, it became apparent to the surgeons and family that amputation was necessary. It was tough but Pat, being blessed with a great attitude and with success written in her story succeeded in her hospital stay by being a real inspiration, and she still is that person. She never said, "woe is me." I love this girl.

Here are some, but by no means, all the accomplishments in Pat's life. She first had to learn to walk again, this time with a prosthesis which is no easy task with all the physical therapy. She finished high school, graduated from college with a degree in education, and taught in public schools until retirement. She learned to alpine ski (most people have trouble doing that on two legs.) She exercises regularly, facilitates writing classes, and uses her talents to bless children with cute bookworms, which she makes. She gives them out freely to encourage young children to read. She is such an inspiration to everyone but especially to those who are physically challenged and might be tempted to use that limitation to do nothing. The world needs more Pats.

Nurse Dorothy Snyder

ACKNOWLEDGMENTS

Appreciation to my writing friends, and authors for their encouragement and understanding in helping me through the journey of writing my memoir. Special thanks to Jaana Hatton, Nancy Miller, who helped me with the basics of writing in the beginning, Judy Weaver, Paula Coomer, and Linda Reid for fine-tuning, and to my editor/publisher, Judi Moreo, for wrapping it all up with a bow on top. Without your assistance, this book would still be in the planning stages.

Thank you to my Writing for Clarity

group for the lessons you taught me about writing from my heart. By sharing our thoughts, we laughed, we cried, and we listened in amazement. There is nothing as special as fellow writers sharing their past. We all have a story that will not only mean something to us for sharing but to our readers who will gain strength knowing they are not alone in their struggles.

Disrupted Expectations

Chapter 1

Entiat High School,
Entiat Washington, 1965/66

On the first day of school, I couldn't believe it was my senior year. Taking extra care with my dark, shoulder-length hair, and makeup, followed by one quick twirl to make sure no slip is showing. All satisfactory, I walked to the top of our dusty driveway and waited for the yellow school bus. Only 179 days left at my lifelong school.

I looked forward to finishing classes, and activities, then walking across the stage to receive my diploma. I wasn't thinking about parting with our close-knit class of forty-five students. Twenty-five graduates had been together for twelve years. Many were off to colleges, universities, and Vietnam. Considering the turmoil in our country during this time, and the uncertainty of whether we would ever see each other again, this added to the apprehension of leaving the safety of home and friends. But the excitement of being on our own overrode that thought.

Skiing Uphill

The year started as usual: new shoes, dresses, PE clothes, a binder full of paper, pencils, markers, and all the usual supplies. Next came the textbooks, which I received with a mental vow to meet every assignment. Expecting graduation requirements to be completed by Christmas, except for History and English, I hoped there was an opening to volunteer in the library or high school office. I looked forward to the blue smudges proving I had been working in either place running off papers on the mimeograph machine. I planned to complete all mandatory classes which would allow time in the choir room to sing and play the piano with the jazz band in preparation for the spring competition in Wenatchee which included all the schools in the immediate area.

The last official school activity was the much-anticipated traditional climb to the top of Numeral Mountain in June. Every senior class claimed their space on the steep, rocky face by painting the number of the year of their graduation, a senior activity that made all parents nervous, but a rite of passage for each class that passed through the halls of Entiat High School. We had to carry on the tradition that started in 1923. Every number translated to "We were

Numeral Mountain

here." To add to the ritual, the junior class had the opportunity to destroy the number within twenty-four hours of completion… another tradition worthy of bragging rights.

With class schedules set, I settled in to enjoy the last year of high school, and the many activities: senior pictures, football, Homecoming, followed by basketball,

Pat West Turner

Pat as Winter Carnival Princess

winter carnival, practice for the winter play, and working as co-editor of the school annual. Other extra-curricular activities included choir and jazz band, various dances, and the much-anticipated Senior Prom.

Classes and activities fell into a routine until the time came to prepare for the last Christmas vacation of my senior year of school. The rehearsals and winter plays were over until we returned in January. As we left school, snow was falling at a blizzard rate, resulting in a heavy build-up of what appeared to be banks of cotton on the landscape. The ride home on the school

Pat & Steve, Co-Editors of the
1966 Annual, "Silico Saska"

Senior Prom Queen 1966

bus was slow.

Heavy accumulations of snow were typical this time of year in northcentral Washington, but weather conditions didn't deter thoughts of going to Wenatchee with friends to officially start Christmas break.

It was two days before Christmas when a classmate, Ron; my best friend, Marietta; my boyfriend, Terry; and I were off to Wenatchee to welcome the first day of freedom from school assignments. Considering the weather, Mother and Dad were discouraging me from going with my friends. I assured them I would be home early. As we left the driveway, they watched the taillights of the car disappear into the blinding snow carrying their only child. I can't even imagine their dread. None of us suspected I wouldn't sleep in my bed for the next three months.

* * * * *

Waking on what felt like a bed of rocks, my sheets soaked with sweat, I couldn't move. The pain was radiating from every pore of my body, my eyes couldn't focus, and my mind was in a fog. What happened!? Where am I? What is going on? So many questions came and went as I fell back into a blissful sleep from the last pain injection.

A person in a white coat stood by my bed and shook me from my drug-induced reprieve from the pain. He identified himself as Dr. Von Smith. He had answers to the few questions my foggy brain asked. The first was, "Why am I here?"

"You have been in a car accident"

This can't be, I was with my friends tonight. That's all the energy I had, and another shot sent me back into blessed sleep, away from any reality and the searing pain.

* * * * *

Awakening again, the bed felt like I was laying on a pile of bricks, and my pillow was soaked with another round of tears and sweat like I was in a sauna. At that time, I didn't know the Lord and wasn't aware I could cry out for mercy.

* * * * *

My determination to go out that night affected my loved ones. Both parents worked full-time jobs as well as a pear and apple orchard to tend to their whole lives. Before and after returning from work, there were animals to care for. Seven days a week, their alarm rang at 4:00 am, and with luck, their heads hit the pillow by 10:00 pm. Sundays were not a day of rest. The home chores still needed to be done, plus preparations for food and clothing for the upcoming week.

My family attended services on Easter and Christmas. To this people made comments, "Oh, it must be Easter/Christmas, the Wests are here." I was young and didn't like those comments then. As an adult, I know how this hurt my mother, but not enough for the family to miss out on these special occasions. Writing this account now makes me sad about how insensitive people can be. If this is what church people are, I didn't want any part of it.

Skiing Uphill

* * * * *

Hours passed; darkness came and went, and there were more injections. An occasional nurse by my side encouraged me to eat, but I refused any food. I wanted everyone and everything to go away, except the nurse with the needle. At night when I heard squeaking soles on the linoleum, I knew the nurse was on her way to ease my pain. During the day, it was too noisy to hear the approaching nurse because of the clanging of metal objects and the conversations of visitors walking down the hall. Nevertheless, with the persistent ringing of my call bell, someone eventually showed me the attention I needed. The thought that kept rolling through my brain during the first days was, "Will there ever be an end to my misery? I didn't want to imagine how many more days I would have to survive like this.

Where is the line between nightmare and reality? Clarity of mind came in fleeting moments. I wondered what the new normal would be, after the wreck, after almost dying, after multiple surgeries, followed by all the drugs. What would life be like going forward? From the day of the accident, December 23, 1965, until I was discharged on March 1, 1966, I experienced many medical and emotional difficulties as did my parents while they watched me experiencing endless days of agonizing pain. My right knee was severely damaged, and the doctors did everything they could to save my leg. The first night after surgery to graft the artery back together after it had been severed, a hard cast was applied. Days later the cast was removed because of the increasing pain. Due to the swelling from trauma, and lack of circulation the side of my calf was severely burned. I had a total of thirteen surgeries due to the burn on the outside of my calf. Even then, the doctors told my parents I would have difficulty walking due to the injury. Looking back, it is a miracle I came out alive and had an ounce of fight left to pick up the pieces of my life. Somehow, I had to find a way to have a life after this nightmare.

New Beginnings

Chapter 2

Nervous laughter, sweaty palms, directions barely heard above the chatter, it was almost time. One last check of my hair and my cap, sitting precariously on my head. My make-up was smudged by tears of joy. After a quick touch-up, and a deep breath, it was time to line up for the drill we had practiced all week. It was show time. The familiar music, Pomp and

Circumstance, started. Voices and laughter from the overflowing audience stopped as the doors to the gym opened. Like soldiers, we marched in a straight line, mostly everyone in step. With the assistance of my walking partner, I was able to maintain my position in the procession. Cameras were clicking as family and friends looked on with pride. I felt excited; I felt scared; I felt nervous and amazed to even be there. The journey to reach this destination was anything but straight, and I don't mean academics only. Walking the length of the gym felt like I was running a marathon due to the amount of pain and effort it took to make my prosthesis perform for each step. But excitement overpowered the pain, and I kept moving forward.

With faltering steps and constant pain, I climbed the stairs to the stage, one by one while maintaining a death grip on the arm of my walking partner, Terry. Reaching the top, we took our seats and listened to teachers and classmates recall our academic accomplishments, and sports awards the basketball team had achieved. Then came encouraging words from our superintendent and it was time for diplomas to be handed out. Graduates' names were called alphabetically. I was one of the last, Patricia Diane West. I dreaded hearing my name because that meant I had to move again. Rising shakily from my seat, I pivoted on the foot I couldn't feel and slowly crossed the stage, unattended with hands outstretched to steady myself like a child first learning to walk. The silence was deafening as I could hear my heart beating with nervousness. Everyone in the audience held their collective breaths with fingers crossed, willing me to reach the lectern a few steps away. Sweat was beading on my forehead while thinking, "I've come this far. I must make it. I can do this." After receiving my diploma, the handshakes, and good luck wishes, I turned again on the lifeless foot and began the long journey back to my seat. Reaching my chair, the audience erupted with applause. Everyone in the room had been instrumental in helping me arrive at this moment. There was not another person in the room who felt as accomplished at that moment as me. I DID IT!

Memories of an Adventurous Childhood

Chapter 3

My childhood was spent seven miles up the Entiat Valley in Washington state. I am an only child, my parent's cherished daughter. We lived in a three-story home that was built by my great-grandfather and had been in our family for three generations. We were a happy family. My parents were untiring workers, always making a safe and secure home. Both sets of grandparents lived nearby, and my aunts, uncles, and cousins gathered often. Life was hard, yet easy. It was hard for my parents to provide food and shelter. My parents and grandparents owned an apple and pear orchard. My parents tended the orchard while both were holding down full-time jobs. They taught me life lessons, by example: how to manage money and time, what a good day's work looked like, and the importance of family.

For me, life was easy. It was uncomplicated. There were no distractions. I had plenty of time to make my adventures and use my imagination. Life was simple, filled with hours outside, spending time with family, and building memories with neighborhood kids.

The house was thirty feet from the edge of the river. Being so close to moving water, there were numerous sounds. During harsh winters, the river froze, blocking the flow upriver. When it melted, the large blocks of ice tumbled by, making scraping sounds on both banks. The eeriest sounds were in the spring when the snow was melting in the mountains causing the water level and volume to increase. The additional current caused the large boulders to roll and grind, making screeching sounds. During the summer, the flow calmed and there was only an occasional splashing against the rocks.

The river provided a swimming hole above my house where the neighbor kids met and swam. In late spring, when the river was still high, we dove from a big rock on the bank. Late one summer, when I went to Girl Scout camp, the river level dropped. When I returned home, I dove off the familiar rock hitting the sandy bottom and splitting the top of my head open. Thankfully, I didn't hit a rock, as I could have easily broken my neck. Friends delivered a crying, sandy, bloody me to my mother and she promptly took me to the doctor who put four stitches on the top of my head. The last stitch secured a round piece of protective gauze. I had recently gotten my shoulder-length hair cut short before going to camp. The doctor said it was a good thing because the shaved part would have been more noticeable. The only safe place for me was at school.

It was pleasant living by the river. In summer, the cottonwood trees lining the riverbank offered shade on hot days. Another benefit, often there was a cool breeze coming off the river. On especially hot days, wading in the cool river was very refreshing. Mother and I sometimes sat on big, flat rocks in mid-stream, and laid back, letting the water wash over the top of us. We had no air conditioning, so the breeze was always welcomed. With the windows open on warm nights, the sudden waft of cool air and the sound of the flowing water were soothing and lulled me to sleep. My water attraction started early and I still find comfort in the sounds and movement of water, whether from the river, lake, or ocean.

The big, old, weathered barn where we stored feed for all the animals also served as a milking barn twice a day. Dad did most of the milking. Occasionally he let me squirt milk to the kittens who anxiously stood by. It was fascinating when the milk was sometimes yellow, instead of white. In the spring when the sunflowers first bloomed, the cows ate the pedals which caused the variation in the color. This was like candy to them following the winter months eating hay and grain. However, when they ate the flowers, their milk tasted bitter, rendering it unusable for a while after we brought them down from the hillside to the pasture where they stayed for the summer months. When the milk became its normal color again, Mother separated the cream and made butter, ice cream, and whipped cream to top pumpkin pies.

The rickety ol' barn was full of surprises. On the main floor, Grandpa kept the antique car that he planned to restore. Unfortunately, he passed before his dream became a reality. The loft had holes so big we had to be incredibly careful not to fall through them when playing in the hay. Mice often scampered about, scaring me only once when I reached into a metal drum for chicken feed to fill my bucket. So as not to be startled again, I made it a habit to give the barrel a vigorous shake before dipping into it. This would give the mice a warning it was time to scat. Because of the mice population, we had several wild barn cats. In time, they learned to trust me as I fed them, and eventually, they would come close enough so I could pet them.

Storing hay in the barn benefitted the deer that roamed the hills behind our orchard. In winter, when the snow was deep and food became hard to find, Grandpa fed the deer at the lower end of the orchard. As soon as the barn door squeaked, the hill came alive as the deer stood and came down to be fed. They had to come across the main road to the upper valley, and it was a miracle none were ever hit. Well, none that

I know of.

When summer came around and the grass dried up in the hills, Dad moved the cows to a friend's pasture that was irrigated. While Dad milked them in the lower pasture, I walked across the road to ride the horse. He was old so I could ride him bareback and without a bridle. One day, he caught a whiff of something across the river, which turned out to be a bear, as indicated by the tracks that were found later, and bucked me off. I landed on the only patch of grass that was surrounded by rocks. That took care of part of my summer as I suffered a hairline fracture of my left hip. I spent most of my time sitting on the floor instead of a chair so I could pet my dog. That all changed as with my injured hip, it was too painful to bend enough to get up. No more sitting on the floor for a while. Luckily, when Dad was home, he was able to lift me by my arms.

I spent most of my summer days playing in the barnyard before I started middle school. I played primarily with the calves. Of all the calves we raised, my favorite was named Blackie. Why did we bond more than the others? It must have been the big brown eyes, and beautiful shiny coat. My first mistake was naming him. My second was making him my playmate. I chased him around in the barnyard, and rode on his back, like a horse until he was too tall and wide. My parents often reminded me not to get too fond of Blackie. When it was time to fill the freezer, I understood what that meant. When I heard the shot, I ran upstairs to my bedroom, flopped down on my bed, and cried. Lesson learned: don't name a food source.

Chasing chickens was also a fun pastime for me. Each spring Mother and Grandma purchased two-hundred baby chicks. When they grew to a certain size, some replaced the old laying hens that became stewing hens. After skillfully cutting the old, and the remainder of the new, chickens into pieces, they were put in the freezer for eating later. Mom made the best chicken and noodles from scratch. I always requested those for my birthday dinner, along with an angel food cake which she also made from scratch. In the group of chickens, occasionally a rooster appeared. One cock-a-doodle-do from him and Grandma made it his last. He quickly joined the other friers in the freezer.

I never got attached to the chickens as I had to Blackie even though they were like toys. It was entertainment chasing them. When they quit laying eggs, Mother knew what I had been up to. Oops, guilty! I needed to find something else to fill my time.

When I wasn't in school, days were filled with playing with the neighbor kids, riding our bikes down our country road, hiking in the hills, and swimming in the river.

Once I had a severe reaction to one of the sprays Dad used to deter bugs from ruining the apples. My face swelled up like a balloon causing my cheeks to crack and I could barely see through the slits of my eyes. When I was older, the dentist explained this was why the enamel on my molars was soft. My reaction to the spray happened at a time when the molars were forming. This was farm life. We didn't know the difference

Living on a farm provided several opportunities for injury. Riding down the hill on a gravel driveway, with our family dog snapping at my bicycle tire, I crashed. The gravel scraped into my knees until I settled in a heap. It took months for that to heal as the gravel worked its way out.

Our vegetable garden was always bountiful. We had so many choices of fresh vegetables for every meal. There were two long rows of tomatoes where I oversaw pulling weeds. The members of the family all spent hours in the kitchen prepping and canning. It was hot, tiring work, but in the winter we had fresh, frozen vegetables from our garden. They complimented the most delicious meals ever. No boxed dinners at our house. The fruit cellar in the basement was packed with our food supply to enjoy during the winter when the ground was covered with snow. The cellar saw an abundance of walnuts after mother picked them up in the orchard. Dad took them to the basement to dry on the floor, in front of our main heat source that filtered up to the second and third floors. When dry, Dad placed them in boxes that were moved to the porch in the summer to crack, pick, and put the nut meat in bags to be stored in the freezer. When we occasionally forgot to cover the box of uncracked nuts, the squirrels helped themselves until we returned. The only food we bought from the grocery store, besides spices, was bacon and ham. Everything else, we raised ourselves. We raised a pig one year and decided it was easier to buy pork products. The sow had a late litter in early winter. We had to put them in a little box and place it by the wood stove in the outer kitchen. I can't remember why, but we had to bottle-feed them. I saw this situation as fun, but the adults saw it as extra work.

The only thing we grew for pleasure were roses. Dad liked the roses. Working in that rose garden was one of the special times Dad and I had together. He taught me where to cut the blooms so more would come and how to keep the insects at bay. He had an array of colors and they smelled so good. We both came away from our time in the roses with little trickles of blood where a thorn had reached out and scratched us. I loved that time with my dad tending his roses.

The local ski hill located above

Skiing Uphill

Ardenvoir, in the Entiat Valley about fifteen miles above my home, had a rope tow that took skiers to the top of the intermediate hill. When I was five, I could not reach the rope. I waited for a tall person to come along. I slid between their skis and held on to their legs. A short way up the hill they stopped and set me free to ski straight down to the bottom where I waited for another tall person.

As I grew taller, I was able to grab onto the rope myself. With this new freedom came the hazard of getting my coat caught. If I clamped my arm too tight, it got tangled in the rope. Clothes back then weren't as form-fitting as they are today. The loose nylon jacket caught in the fibers of the rope and as the rope twisted, my coat twisted with it. I wasn't aware until my gloved hands tried to let go. This action resulted in a frantic, jerky ride through the safety gate. My ski tripped the safety wire, and that broke the electrical circuit, and stopped the tow from moving. To remedy the problem, I learned to hold tight with my hands, rather than under my armpit.

We had a lodge with a large, floor-to-ceiling rock fireplace. Before eating lunch, we stood in front of the warm fire to thaw our frozen hands and dry our wet clothes.

Most of our ski pants and sweaters were made of wool that steamed as they dried. Luckily, the aroma of Les's delicious burgers sizzling on the grill was stronger than the smell of wet wool. After warming up enough for our hands to thaw, and clothes to dry, it was time for lunch. Along with a Les Burger, we also had the option of a cold drink called a Graveyard. This was a concoction Les developed, by adding a mixture of all the flavors from the soda fountain.

Every Wednesday the hill opened for night skiing. Only the intermediate hill had lights. Parents turned their kids loose and we became one big family. Many eyes were watching to see where and how fast we were going. When the moon was full, we could see the terrain on the more advanced hill. Only then did kids and adventuresome adults escape through the trees to experience the steeper slope. At the side of that hill was a ski jump, but no one I know was ever brave enough to fly off the ramp into the unknown darkness.

Skiing was a social event, as I made many new friends who shared the love of this winter sport. A friend of my parents, Otto, gave me ski lessons. When I was twelve years old, he taught me skills that made skiing more enjoyable. Besides improving my skiing skills, Otto also saved my emotional life years later.

I have such wonderful memories of growing up. I wouldn't change my life for the world. I always felt secure and loved.

Lessons Learnedly

Chapter 4

As an adult, I understand how the events of my childhood prepared me for what was to come. I was raised on a farm, I knew the meaning of life, loss, injuries, and death. My first experience with loss happened when the Entiat River road was straightened. The new section of the road split our fruit orchard in half. That highway was not a benefit for us, because of the extra work it made for my parents working the fruit in two different areas.

As the road was being constructed the orchard trucks and machinery went back and forth across the road, and my pet dogs would follow. Four of my pets were killed by speeding drivers on the new, straight road, even before it was paved. Skipper, my cocker spaniel, was the first. I'm glad my parents told me, rather than letting me see her lifeless body. I was devastated, as being an only child, she was my playmate. She even shared the poison oak oil she collected on her long, reddish hair. All summer no matter what dog we had, I always had bumps in the crooks of my arms from carrying them around. Within a week, of losing Skipper, we were walking through the orchard early one morning, when we heard whimpering and found a small cocker puppy. I wonder if it was put there by the person who hit my dog, or by my parents.

When I started kindergarten, both of my parents worked so they left home early. Mother always packed me a warm piece of cinnamon toast and drove me to my best friend, Marietta's, home so her mother could watch after me while we waited for the bus. When it was time, the two of us walked by ourselves to the top of her long driveway and waited for the yellow bus to pick us up. At noon, the same bus returned us to her home where I waited for Mother's return. That was the routine for a couple of years until I was old enough to walk to the top of my driveway alone.

As Mother waved good-by each morning, she assured me, "I love you. Be a good girl. I'll pick you up after work." Because of her job, she didn't drive me to school. No holding my hand to guide me to the new kindergarten classroom. I remember standing in front of the ominous brick school building, with the steep cement steps leading to the entrance. Not knowing where to go and being afraid of the big people walking around me, I stood outside crying. A couple of high school girls came to my rescue and took me down the steep stairs to my new classroom.

I remember the first day of kindergarten and my new dress, shoes, green rug for rest time, and an armload of school supplies, especially the new box of crayons. I earned money to buy the supplies by gathering and cleaning glass pop bottles which we saved in apple boxes outside by the garage. Each bottle was worth a penny. Doing this job was especially difficult for me, as each bottle contained at least one dried-up spider. I wasn't then, and I'm still not, a bug person! The challenge of managing the bottles and completing the task was worth every penny. I was proud of that thirty-six-count box of crayons.

The weather was warm in September when school started, and by the time I arrived home that first day, my new dress was wrinkled, shiny new shoes were scuffed, and my feet had matching blisters on each heel, casualties from playing outside during recess. As soon as I got home, I immediately took off my school clothes and replaced them with familiar summer play clothes. Summer was a time of shorts and going barefoot, and I missed them both already.

During the first month of third grade, the bus driver chose me to stand in front, next to him. When he stopped to pick up the children, I opened and closed the manual door. Then we continued down the valley to the long, red brick, elementary school building in Entiat, Washington. Normally, we got in trouble for standing up in a moving bus, but that was my job until automatic doors were installed. The only means of protection that anchored me to my station was a metal pole. I held on with determination. My hands were small, and my fingers didn't quite reach all the way around. By the time we arrived at school, my knuckles were white from gripping so hard.

Being trusted with that responsibility at such an early age was the start of many character-building experiences. I'm sure the driver would have chuckled if he had known I took my job so seriously. Years later, I realized this experience helped prepare me for what was ahead.

Five miles above my home was Cooper's General Store, located in Ardenvoir, WA. Cooper's had a variety of miscellaneous items of hardware that often saved a trip to Wenatchee, which was thirty miles away when an unexpected repair was needed. This store was a benefit for me because of the grocery store attached. Each day the Wonder Bread truck made deliveries of packaged bread, Twinkies, Sno Balls, and other treats. Before long, I looked forward to seeing the familiar truck coming toward me. When the vehicle popped around the corner, I quickly learned he had finished deliveries early and was going to pass by my driveway, ahead of the school bus. He often stopped and gave me a mini loaf of white Wonder Bread, or a single wrapped

Twinkie or Sno Ball. It was a good day when I put extra treats in my lunch box.

Amazing how I survived the first years without my parent's home-to-school delivery or a cell phone. But I did, and suddenly, thirteen years later, I was once again waiting for the yellow bus (a newer model.)

The school years flew by. I was a senior looking forward to no more rides on the bus, no jumping to the sound of school bells, or sitting through classes taught by the same teachers who taught my parents when they were in school.

Dark Memories

Chapter 5

Driving in snowstorms can be extremely dangerous. That explains why two days before Christmas my parents had reason to worry. Earlier I mentioned going to Wenatchee at the beginning of Christmas vacation. Despite the storm becoming a whiteout, we arrived safely in Wenatchee. All available snow removal equipment was in service, attempting to keep the city streets passable, thus forming high snow berms down the middle of all lanes. One large grader that was in service to remove snow had tire chains draped over the orange reflecting strips on the back of the vehicle, blocking any visible signs of warning. As the vehicle stopped to turn into the Department of Transportation lot on Wenatchee Avenue, it happened. Through the darkness, and in the blinding blanket of snow, the back of a large object suddenly appeared in front of us like a stone wall.

At that moment, I lost three days of my life. I have scattered memories of the day before, the day of, and the day after the car accident. I can only share what my parents and friends told me in detail about what happened in those three days.

I am thankful those days were blocked from my memory. I don't recall the split second I realized we were going to crash into a very large, unknown object or the sudden jolt, and then the sound of crunching metal. There were screams of pain before shock enveloped our bodies. There was a moment of silence while the snow started covering the violent scene. On-lookers were trying to comprehend what they were seeing. No one knew what was behind the crumpled doors. Is it possible anyone was alive? My new orange corduroy jacket was slowly turning crimson.

There were no seatbelts in our car, as seatbelts had not been installed in all cars at the time. Plus, the Corvair we were riding in had windows made of authentic glass. If we had been farther away from the hospital and emergency crews, my best friend and I might not have survived. With our severe injuries, we could easily have bled out on the spot. It was a miracle the ambulance could reach us as it maneuvered through the snow and the slow-moving traffic. Many cars were stuck in the piles of snow the plows had left in the middle of the street. There were no cell phones, and other lines of communication were down because of the heavy, wet snow hanging on the telephone wires overhead. To this day, I don't know who contacted someone to get help or even how they did it.

The injuries we received were physical, emotional, and life-changing. Marietta was sitting in the front bucket seat. On impact, she was thrown through the windshield, shattering the glass with her face and head. She received additional lacerations as she bounced back through the broken glass, before landing in her seat. Later, the surgeon told her he stopped counting at eight hundred stitches. During surgery, the doctor discovered that her optic nerve was partially severed. She also had defensive cuts on her arms from attempting to avoid what was coming toward her.

The driver, Ron, was thrown forward by the abrupt stop. The steering wheel broke on impact. He received a broken arm, broken ribs, and lacerations to his chest. Terry, sitting next to me in the back seat, suffered a broken arm and dislocated shoulder.

I had my feet under the driver's seat. On impact, I was thrown forward, settling in the cramped space on the floorboard in front of the passenger's bucket seat. The initial position of my feet and the forward motion caused my left hip to dislocate, and the right knee to compound dislocate. To understand my injury, stretch your leg straight out in front of you, bring your toe straight back, and touch your nose. That is what happened to my leg. I was yelling and crying as the ambulance crew had difficulty freeing me because I was crammed in a most unnatural position in the confined space, not to mention my broken or dislocated limbs. To this day, I have no memory of my horrific injuries or pain that night. It was a moment in time I thankfully missed.

As we were tossed so violently, we all had concussions, contributing to our memory loss.

Arriving at the hospital, Marietta was immediately rushed to surgery. The attendants were working feverously to contain the bleeding from her head lacerations. While the others were receiving medical attention in the emergency room, I waited in the hall on the ambulance gurney. When the extent of my leg injury was noticed, I was also rushed off to surgery to repair my severed artery.

While I waited, I gave the admitting staff our contact information: names, parents' names, birth dates, phone numbers, etc. Considering the state of shock, I was in, I'm surprised everything I told them was accurate, except for my birthday.

The phone call followed… the one all parents dread receiving in the middle of the night. Their child was in an accident. To reach the hospital, our parents had to drive thirty miles in the same snowstorm that caused our accident. In the small town of Entiat, news spread quickly.

As I waited my turn for treatment, a nurse stopped to take my vitals. My pulse and blood pressure were dropping. Earlier, the staff had not discovered that the artery in the back of my right knee had been severed from the compound dislocation. With every beat of my heart, blood was seeping out. They immediately rushed me to surgery. It was necessary to take an artery from my left groin to reattach the blood flow to my right knee.

All factors considered, despite the wreck, conditions, severity of injuries, and available medical treatments, it wasn't my time to leave this earth. I didn't have a relationship with God at that time, but now I know He was with me then and brought me through this life-changing trauma. Looking back, I see the path that was set for my life that night. How many people can say without a doubt, "I know why this happened"? Never was I angry nor did I blame anyone, let alone God, for my situation.

You can imagine my confusion as I woke in the recovery room with excruciating pain in every part of my body. I could not move because of the cast on my leg and my drug-induced, foggy mind. Soon I learned I had been in a car wreck. Then I drifted back into a fitful, sweaty sleep, not realizing I was fighting for my life.

My immediate need was to survive. I was tended to by an expert team of specialists:

surgeon, Dr. Stojowski; vascular surgeon, Dr. Jerry Gibbons; and orthopedic surgeon, Dr. Von Smith. Their immediate focus was to put me back together. The Deaconess Hospital was my home for the next three months, and I am forever grateful for the staff responsible for my care.

In the following months, I found out what determination felt like.

The Challenges of Healing

Chapter 6

The timeline surrounding events that happened during the first month in the hospital is not clear in my memory. What is clear was a most uncomfortable hospital bed contributed to my horrendous pain. It was hard to tell if the source of pain came from the initial injuries or the treatment on my leg.

Being tossed around in the car resulted

in many points of injury. No one impact was less painful than the next. The sudden blow to my head caused a large hematoma above my right temple and a severe concussion. The dislocated left hip and compound dislocated right knee were equally painful as was the back of my right knee where my artery had been reconnected. The hard cast that had been applied to secure everything in place caused another level of pain. I compare the pain to what I have experienced when visiting the dentist. Regardless of breathing nitrous gas, I still felt the pain but didn't jerk away. In the first days after the accident, no amount of pain meds took the edge off my suffering. On a scale of one to ten, the level of pain was fifteen. I saw no end to this nightmare.

The pain continued to intensify as the days passed. It was apparent something was wrong. First, the doctors considered it might be the hard cast on my leg. They were surprised at what they saw when the cast was cut off. On the entire side of my calf was a sizeable, severe burn. Due to the initial trauma, surgery, lack of circulation, and restriction from the hard cast, my entire lower leg had swollen, adding to the pressure, burning, and pain. The doctors told me it looked red and angry. I had no desire to look at my mangled limb. Not only was I an accident victim, but also a burn patient. Treatment for that required the dying skin to be removed by debriding. The pain continued to be controlled by the heaviest medication, but the reprieves never lasted more than three hours. And waiting for the required fourth hour to pass before I could have more pain medication kept the nightmare going.

In my unending discomfort, the rancid smell of rotting tissue surrounding me was disgusting. Every few days, a trip to surgery was required so the doctors could remove the dying flesh. In total, this procedure required twelve surgeries, all under sedation. The sedation always upset my entire system causing me to throw up, which added to the never-ending discomfort and weakness.

The day before each tissue removal, I was wheeled to physical therapy. My entire body was immersed in a tub full of warm water. This softened the surrounding skin, allowing the dying area to be easier to cut away. I looked forward to the times in the tub. If you have ever been in the hospital for any length of time and endured sponge baths you understand what I am talking about. Oh, the feeling of submerging my entire body in a tub of warm water was wonderful. The feeling of floating, and the warmth of the water allowed my body to relax from the continual tension throughout since the day of the accident.

The doctors felt hopeful about saving my leg. During morning rounds, they asked me to wiggle my toes. This would be a sign the nerves were starting to grow back. As hard as I tried, I couldn't even wiggle my big toe.

Before long, I became aware of another simple pleasure of hospital life. I couldn't wait for the day I was mobile enough to use the commode instead of a bed pan.

Unfortunately, that was weeks in coming.

Early in the evening after the twelfth surgery to remove dead tissue, the doctor came into my room and gave me the news. Barely awake from sedation administered earlier that day, I heard him say, "Pat, we need to amputate your leg." I knew something was wrong, so I wasn't surprised as I had been getting weaker and weaker, sicker, and sicker. I was so tired, and sick by that time, I didn't care. The days were endless, consisting of sleep and drugs. I would have consented to anything to stop the rancid smell and the pain.

I knew the doctors had done everything

in their power to save my leg. Now, I had to trust them again, with my life and my fate. As the doctor spoke to my parents in the darkened room, I didn't comprehend anything after "gangrene, amputation, blah, blah, blah..." The hardest part of that day was seeing my parents cry. The doctor told them to go home and rest in preparation for the next day as it was going to be a long one.

My parents knew it was time to go when the nurse came to prep me for the next day, waving an object while announcing. "It's time for your enema, Pat." That was one way to clear a room. The nurse's announcement was one more thing to add to the lengthy list of circumstances over which I had no control. When that process was complete, another nurse came in to shave my thigh. I asked her, "Please shave my other leg, too." I saw her nod in the dim light. It had been a long time, and even in my weakened state, I wanted to do anything that might make me feel better. I compare that to something I mentioned earlier about being immersed in the tub of water. Physical or emotional pain, both were the same. I felt helpless because my life, movements and location were not of my choosing.

Early the next morning, my bed was

pushed down the brightly lit hallway into the operating room. In the cold, sterile environment stood the anesthesiologist I had come to know well. "Please let this be my last surgery."

As he was preparing to put me to sleep, I heard the murmuring voices and the sound of metal instruments of the surgical staff being arranged on a tray close by. I am thankful I didn't hear or see the saw that would soon separate part of my leg from my body. As I drifted to sleep, I had no idea what the events of the next months would have in store for me, and at that point, I didn't care.

Skiing Uphill

The surgery lasted eighteen hours. In the recovery room, I started bleeding from the open end of what was now my stump. In surgery, as the vessel was cut, it snapped out of sight, back inside before it was tied off. Now, I had a bleeder. A tourniquet was applied to stop the flow of blood. More breathtaking pain as the constricting band was slipped over what was left of my thigh. When it kept bleeding, they returned me to surgery and I was put under sedation for the second time that day. More throwing-up to come.

For the next few days, I remained in the drug-induced fog. I remember thinking,

"How can people function and use drugs at the same time?" Now, I know. They can't.

Weeks before the amputation, a variety of trained staff were doing their best to help pull me through my injuries. I was so young, with so many emotional and medical needs, several of them became attached, something they were warned against in nurses' training. But some had daughters my age, and their reality was that this could happen to them. By this time, I had been there for a month of what became my three-month stay.

Beyond their concern and physical attention, the staff saw my determination to heal. Because of the amputation, they felt they had let me down. My reality was that they had not failed, but had kept me alive, both emotionally and physically. I was no longer a patient they had casually met. Everyone on the surgical floor was sad about what was in store. The ones on duty the morning of my amputation stood by their stations and cried as I wheeled past them, down the hall, on my way to surgery. They knew it was going to be a long day and my life would be forever changed.

When they removed the source of septic infection that had been draining into my system, and I started coming down from high doses of pain medications, I became more aware of my surroundings. Because of my critical condition, I was moved into a private room with round-the-clock care. The first few nights after the accident, Marietta's sister, and sister-in-law, who were both in the nursing program at the hospital, volunteered their time to stay and watch over both Marietta and me.

Dark and Light Moments

Chapter 7

After the amputation, every day seemed the same, yet different. I lived for nurses coming through the door with a hypodermic syringe. I knew that relief was soon to be, even though short-lived. My body relaxed in the warmth and sleep, however fitful. Waiting for the next shot started long before the four hours passed. The liquid diet was untouched. Bedpans were necessary, but another painful challenge. At first, there were no curtains open to let the sunlight in. My room was as dark as my mood and as bleak as my future. The doctor's updates sounded like, "Blah, Blah, Blah, See you tonight." The sign over my bed disappeared, which read, "I didn't think it would get worse, then it did."

During the first 48 hours, no one knew if I was going to survive. Dad had to leave the hospital during this critical time to drive my grandmother to Seattle to catch a plane. She needed to be with my aunt who was having surgery the next week. The snow had not quit falling for days, so local roads and mountain passes were treacherous. While remaining to sit with me, Mother didn't trust that Dad would safely return from his trip over the passes covered with heavy accumulations of snow. To this day, I regret the hell I put my parents through by making a stupid teenage choice to leave the house in a snowstorm.

Once my dad returned from Seattle, neither one EVER missed a day coming to see me for the three months. Dad worked twenty-five miles from the hospital at the rail station in Entiat, tallying lumber before it was lifted onto the train. Mother worked in the apple industry as a supervisor in a packing shed in Wenatchee only blocks away.

After the workday, Dad rode to town with a co-worker, then he and Mother rode home together late each night. On the weekends, both stayed with me all day.

I was totally at the mercy of the medical staff. To change positions so I could raise or lower my head, I needed someone to turn the crank at the end of my bed. After the night nurses finished getting other patients ready for bed, one would always come back to check on me. After checking my vitals and pain level, they often gave me a back rub using powder or lotion. Before moving on, they cranked the bed flat, and said, "Good night." I wouldn't see them again until I used my call button, indicating the time for pain medication.

During the day, to break my boredom of the lack of a television or a telephone, because that was usually out of my reach, the nurses used their break time to wheel me to physical therapy for a change of scenery. My only other distraction was a goldfish that a classmate, Julie, brought to my bedside. I spent hours watching it swim around and around in its bowl, top to bottom, side to side, and back again. I began to wonder if I was watching what my life was going to be, swimming in circles to nowhere, trapped. When the nurses applied antiseptics to my wound, a mist potentially covered the water and might affect the goldfish, so they moved it across the room to the sink. The nurses didn't want me to lose anything else, not even a goldfish.

For weeks after the amputation, I couldn't look at the heavily bandaged stump. It was hard enough glancing at the bump under the sheets. I knew my leg was gone, so when the sheets were changed, I diverted my eyes. One day, it was exceptionally warm, and I threw off the sheet. There it was. No, there it wasn't.

Looking at my stump for the first time, I froze and got sick to my stomach.

All medications for pain, IV fluids, vitamins, antibiotics, and whatever else my body needed were administered directly into my hips. No piggyback IV system for injections. After weeks of pokes in my hips, they became unnaturally hard. The nurses had to be ready to cover the area with a cotton ball as soon as the needle was removed, or liquid spewed out like a geyser. By this time, I knew which nurses were good at injections, and which were not. An older nurse was not allowed back in my room for the way she gave the shots.

Instead of giving a quick poke and push, she pricked the skin then slowly pushed the needle in, then the medication. Wow, I didn't need that.

The food was okay, but I couldn't eat. It took time to get back my sense of taste and desire to eat because of the infection that had been circulating through my blood, plus medications and inactivity. I didn't realize how hungry I was until Louie, a classmate from school started smuggling in Dusty burgers stuffed in his pocket. It didn't matter that they were mashed with filling oozing out inside the wrapping. They tasted so good. To give you an idea of my lack of appetite, on the day of the accident, I weighed 175 pounds. The day I left the hospital, three months later, I weighed 113 pounds. I do not recommend this weight loss program.

The memory that haunts me more than the amputation is how I reacted to my family when I hit the 'angry' stage of grief from loss. For hours, Mother sat by my bedside. I didn't speak or make eye contact with her or anyone else that came into the sterile room. This went on for at least two weeks. Years later, I told her how sorry I was. She looked puzzled and said she had no memory of that happening. I am thankful I apologized before she passed away. My parents went through an array of emotions while watching me twist in pain day after day with one physical challenge stacked on another and no end in sight. During that depression period, she got permission to bring my dog, Mitzi, into my room in hopes of lifting my spirits. The power of my mother's unconditional love still brings tears to my eyes.

I spent Christmas, New Year, my eighteenth birthday on February 6th, and Valentine's Day confined in the hospital. Everyone in my small hometown knew and grieved when something happened to members of the community, especially the kids. It does take a village to raise a child. Get well cards poured in daily, filling the wide windowsill in my room. They surprised me on Valentine's Day with a 'card shower' including encouraging notes and money. When I finished opening my mail I had over 150 dollars surrounding me on my bed.

A local beautician friend came in, washed my waist-length hair, and styled it beautifully up on my head for my eighteenth birthday. Getting my hair washed didn't happen often, so that was a great present. Also, for my birthday, a club I belonged to

Pat West Turner

*Eighteenth birthday in the hospital
with parents*

at school brought me a large, pink, shaggy stuffed dog.

Starting the night of the accident, and during hospitalization, I needed many units of blood. Volunteers from the community donated blood to the local blood bank replacing the units I used, so my parents would not be charged. The community helped me yet another time. When I healed enough to be measured for a prosthesis, they organized a benefit clam feed. Community members drove to Seattle and brought back fresh clams. Enough money was donated to buy my first prosthesis. This was long before the computerized, and sports legs of today. To give an idea of inflation, my first leg cost $900.00. Three decades later, the same basic leg cost $30,000.

After numerous trips to surgery, I became friends with the anesthesiologist. I'm not sure how he was always there for me, but that's enough to call him a friend. When he came to say goodbye, I told him I wouldn't be back to even have a baby!! He smiled.

Five years later, I returned with appendicitis. This was not a convenient time as I had started my September experience required before student teaching to finish my BA degree. Somehow, I put in enough days earlier, so I began student teaching on time. Yes, I let everyone know I was NOT happy about being there. Multiple times staff asked, "Did I have anything to eat or drink" to which I emphatically said, "NO." The anesthesiologist asked one more time before he put me to sleep for surgery. Later he told me, I popped up on one elbow and said, "I'm glad everyone is happy that I'm hungry and I'm thirsty." To that, he said, "Oh, Pat, go to sleep," as he gently laid me down. He said I came out of the anesthetic mad, too. Unfortunately, I've had more procedures than I can count requiring his services, and he still smiles when I come through the surgical doors.

It's a wonder I don't have nightmares of that tragic time in my young life. I am thankful the memories of the three months in the hospital have faded. The years to follow have held additional physical challenges and yet, I'm here to share my not-so-straight journey. Now when asked, "How are you doing?" I continue to reply: "I'm in good shape for the shape I'm in."

The Rough Road to Recovery

Chapter 8

When my leg was amputated, they took as little bone as possible. The doctors knew a long stump made it easier to control the prosthesis. There wasn't enough tissue to fold together to suture, allowing a strong bond. Shortly after the initial amputation, the raw end was prepared for skin grafts. To prepare the site for the new skin, the nurses wrapped the stump with bandages soaked in a solution that smelled like an Italian salad. The mixture was supposed to help the new skin attach easier to the open wound. The grafting skin was cut into thin strips taken from my left thigh. The nerves, barely below the surface were exposed which caused more pain and required stronger drugs.

On the day of the surgery, the doctors placed the thin layers from my left thigh side-by-side over the exposed bone, which allowed no room for additional padding on the rounded end of my stump. With that done, there was more pain while I waited to heal.

Skiing Uphill

When the skin on my thigh where the skin was shaved off was no longer raw, I prematurely went without a protective bandage. The first night going without protection I broke open the tender skin while rolling over in bed and rubbing against the crisp sheet. I realized I needed that barrier a while longer. I can't even imagine what burn victims experience.

By now, it was the last of February of my senior year of high school. Time for the high school state basketball tournaments to begin. Entiat had a winning record through the regular season. The team was comprised mostly of seniors...my classmates. This was important for players, our school, and me. Successful through district playoffs, we were on our way to the state championship games in Spokane, WA … everyone except me. I was still in the hospital. The school even closed for the occasion. I desperately wanted to go but when I asked my doctors, they collectively said "No" repeatedly. They said I was too fragile after the first amputation, and susceptible to infection. The last thing they wanted was to disrupt the skin grafts, but I knew I had to go! Slowly slipping into a state of depression, my vital signs, and any strength I had regained weakened. My deteriorating condition finally caught the doctor's attention. At last, the answer I needed to hear was, "Yes, you can go under three conditions: your parents take you, make time to rest, and take your antibiotics." With a resounding "YES," I was soon discharged and went out the door for what I hoped would be the last time.

It was March 1 of 1966, and I headed home, not because I was physically ready

Hospital staff at Deacones Hospital,
Wenatchee, Washington

to leave the hospital, but because of the basketball team. Being free from tubes, needles, and medical staff did more for my emotional and physical healing than any medicine. The team didn't take first place, but for me, it was the trip of a lifetime, and they were my ticket to freedom. After the district games, I went back to school and made up for the three months I had lost. Luckily, I only needed credits in English and Math. Mother took me to school in the morning, then after the two periods, she left work and took me back home, so I could rest.

I entered another time of waiting to

heal. After the doctors said the end was healed, I was refitted with a newly shaped socket. Within days, putting my stump in the prosthesis became increasingly painful. Half of the skin graft had attached, and the other half had not. The fluid that leaked from the open wound during the day crusted over at night. Every morning, when I put my prosthesis on, the crust broke apart. The first step felt like I had stepped on a knife.

The Monday after receiving my high school diploma, I returned to the hospital where doctors re-amputated and took an additional four inches of bone from my stump, leaving enough skin to fold over and stitch. This caused another delay in my healing.

I hoped that would be the last time I would darken the doors of the hospital, but it wasn't. Days after returning home, I developed a high fever. While in the hospital for the re-amputation, I picked up a hospital staph infection, so back to the hospital I went. I spent two weeks recovering on what the nurses called the "heart attack" floor with a drain tube inserted in the end of my already sensitive stump. Because of the staph infection, I was not allowed on the medical floor where I knew all the nurses.

The reason was to protect other patients who had recently had surgery. They were more vulnerable to infections, especially the kind I had. I missed the surgical floor team I had spent so many months with, but I understood.

Back at home again I began to swim as soon as the incision where the tube was inserted healed. Since I had contracted a staph infection, I wasn't allowed in public pools, for the safety of other swimmers, as well as myself. My uncle had an above-ground pool that he graciously helped my dad set up in our backyard for the remainder of the summer. Finally, I had a feeling of normalcy. I spent hours floating around, recovering. Before I knew it, fall was approaching, and it was time to prepare for college.

This last setback left little time for my stump to heal, get refitted with a new socket on my prosthesis, and practice walking before I started college. Beyond hope, this was another of many more challenges to come.

First Survive, Then Thrive

Chapter 9

It is a miracle I survived, but then what? I had no intentions of going to college upon completion of high school. The school counselor discouraged me. Plus, I had a boyfriend, so marriage and kids seemed more likely. All that changed. Three months in the hospital was a long time re-think my future.

Feeling I had already lost control of

my life, I didn't want to depend on anyone other than the hospital staff to take care of me. Because of all the medical trauma I had been through, a new plan developed. I decided to go to college, but how was I to financially achieve this? Most may not think it was a blessing to have lost a leg, but that's exactly what it turned out to be. Because of my physical, "substantial impediment" regarding my ability to work, I qualified for federally funded vocational rehabilitation.

My parents would have found a way to help me go to college, but the program helped relieve some of the financial burdens. The trauma of my accident was already a hardship they had experienced, including the expenses of many trips to Seattle, often staying for days while my new leg was being constructed or the old one repaired. I didn't want to add to all that.

People around me were trying to be realistic and helpful by telling me what I could, should, or would not be able to do. For example, the words of my high school counselor, "You don't need to worry about college because you're not smart enough," kept running through my mind during the months in the hospital. Such discouraging comments became frustrating and confusing as the list got longer with outside, unsolicited advice. My self-esteem was bruised by the fear they might be right. Self-doubt grew. I wondered if I was good for anything. Would anyone take me seriously? Was marriage in my future? The unknown started playing with my mind. At one time I thought there was nothing I couldn't do. The immediate milestone was to heal, walk, and graduate from high school. Yet, the struggles and challenges continued to increase my self-doubt.

After deciding to go to college, the most nagging question became, "How am I going to walk from one end of the campus to the other?" Not being steady enough, I was still using a cane. In addition to my physical challenges, I had emotional fears to overcome, with being different. But like Christmas, the beginning of college came whether I was ready or not. The doctors helped me survive, now it was up to me to thrive.

Despite all the doubts and fears from the beginning of my new life, at the age of eighteen, giving up was never an option. During my childhood when illness, challenges, loss of loved ones, or even beloved pets occurred, I witnessed people "picking themselves up by their bootstraps and moving on." This was a common phrase from my grandma that kept resonating with me. Ok, this is what happened, I have no one to blame but myself, now, what am I going to do about it? My life was saved for a reason, there must be something good to come from all of this. I chose not to let anything stop me now.

Lessons Learned

Chapter 10

From the day of the accident until I was discharged from the hospital, I had many medical and emotional difficulties. Looking back, I recognized the medical miracle the hospital team had performed. The bigger miracle was that I had an ounce of fight left in me to pick up the pieces of my life.

The first lesson learned by my medical team: Don't put a hard cast on a newly injured limb. By the time my leg had to be amputated, I was so ill I was afraid I was going to die and afraid I wasn't. What appeared to be my biggest hurdle was only the beginning of a long road to recovery.

The second lesson was the one learned by the nursing staff: Don't become emotionally attached to the patient. Because of their attachment, they felt they had failed me when my leg was surgically removed. To me, their emotional attachment gave them more reason to care for all my needs, not only my physical condition. Because of their care, I was still alive.

The rest of the lessons I learned. I

got upset with the nurses, even though I knew they were following doctors' orders. Because I was going in and out of extreme pain with each medical challenge, I had frequent doses of morphine. As I recovered from each new trauma, I started receiving pain pills instead of injections. I was not happy. I learned from experience that I preferred injections, as painful as they were, for immediate relief as opposed to the oral medication that took at least half of an hour to deaden anything, and relief didn't last as long.

After leaving the safety of the hospital, I had numerous experiences that could have been my undoing. Not only was I learning how to live on one leg I also struggled with a new perception of myself. It didn't help my raw feelings when people jerked their children away when asked, "Mommy, what happened to her?" The reactions to my appearance reinforced the feeling that I was broken. I was especially aware of the stares from classmates when I returned to finish my senior year. Since pants were not allowed in school except on exceptionally cold winter days, and this was May, I had no choice but to wear dresses. Even though I wore nylons, my artificial limb still looked like a Barbie doll leg. I learned it was up to me how I reacted to other people's perceptions of me.

Sitting in the waiting room for yet another doctor's appointment, I had the sweetest encounter with a toddler. It was a warm summer day, and I was wearing shorts. My Barbie knee caught the eye of the little girl. She was not walking on her own yet, so she inched her way toward me by holding onto the chairs. She didn't take her eyes off my knee. Out of the corner of my eye, I could see the nervousness in her mother. What impressed me is that the mother didn't try to stop her child. As the little one got close enough, she reached out and touched my knee. Then she patted it, looked up at me, and using her limited vocabulary, she said, "Oh, pretty." I glanced toward her mother, smiled, and said, "It's been called a lot of things, but never pretty." She smiled as relief washed over her face. This encouraged me to think the leg could be viewed as pretty, but not yet. I knew that one day, I would have to make friends with it.

Before starting back to class, I healed enough to start the fitting process for my wooden leg. On the first of April 1966, Mother and I started trips to Seattle. At the time, this was the closest prosthetic facility. During the initial visit, I received a shrinker sock to force fluid out of my stump before the initial casting of my remaining thigh. Although uncomfortable from the constriction, I was willing to do anything to have two feet again. We returned home and waited. It was a slow process like everything else at that time. FRUSTRATION!

On our next trip, a technician measured my stump and made a mold using a Plaster of Paris material. First, a mesh stocking was applied, then the wet plaster was molded around the entire stump, paying close attention to the groin area. This is the most sensitive besides the end of the stump, as both have little padding from muscle or fat layers. This step had to be repeated until the fit was right. The stump kept changing as a result of shrinkage from tissue constriction in the hard socket. It also swelled or shrank depending on weight gain or loss. When the fit felt good, something would change, and it didn't. Then I went through the process of making a new cast of my stump, and fitting steps again. This caused yet another opportunity to practice more patience and deal with disappointment.

Changing the dynamics of the socket caused more discomfort because of additional pressure in the groin area. I had a built-in barometer for weight that only allowed five pounds one way or the other. The groin area was sensitive to pressure. From this, I discovered I had internal stitches that were supposed to have dissolved but hadn't. The rubbing caused a boil-like cyst that had to be surgically removed. Another delay in healing, costing me more precious time for walking practice.

Finally, a trip back to Seattle for the last of the socket fittings. With a satisfactory fit, it was time to choose a knee unit, friction, or hydraulic. I chose the hydraulic for faster reaction time, allowing my stride to be smooth. There were setbacks with this type of knee unit: when the seal broke, hydraulic fluid leaked, making a gushing sound, and the knee swung freely. The only way to fix it was to return to Seattle to replace the unit.

Another choice was the height of the heel; One inch or flat. I chose an inch, thinking about when I dressed up. I was eighteen and appearance was important. Before the accident, I had many pairs of shoes. Afterward, it was difficult to find the right heel height and means to hold the shoe on.

Yet, another focus needed to change. This one turned out to my advantage, and finally a break. To fill the place of shoes, I discovered I have a standard ring-size finger. Settling for this substitute of enjoyment, I have acquired quite an array of rings over the years since then.

I did everything I could think of to detract from my bionic leg which turned out to be a losing battle! In the beginning, I had a love/hate relationship with this block of wood! Once the two pieces were screwed or glued into place, I took it home for a trial run with this newly constructed leg and a much-needed rest. I was determined to make friends with this foreign-looking thing that was becoming an extension of me. When the trial run was successful, we traveled the three hours and spent more nights in Seattle while the leg was being completed by the technician and to my satisfaction. This required applying layers of lamination to reinforce the joints and spray-painting it a skin tone close to my own.

We returned home late from Seattle, and I planned to start the trial period when waking in the morning. I slid out of the socket and sat the leg in the corner by my bed. Immediately, the leg toppled and crashed to the floor. I looked in horror at the two pieces before me. The parts had broken exactly where the knee had been temporarily glued.

Despite this disaster, early the next day I had an appointment for a fitting with a friend of my mother who was a seamstress and was making my clothes at the time. I was self-conscious and did everything I could to not draw attention to the outline at the top of my artificial leg which showed through my dresses and skirts. She had a way of minimizing that hard-line near my hip. When I started to tell her, what happened at home, I became tearful again. My mother's friend replied firmly, "Pat, I thought you were stronger than that." The powerful statement will forever be etched in my memory. To this day, every challenge brings back her words. I thought over time these words would soften, but they haven't. Am I weak? I survived so many challenges and setbacks after my accident, this can't be true. It was hard to understand why she perceived me as weak. There were so many mixed messages, I started to doubt myself again. "Why is everything so difficult?" The reality was that I had come too far to let her words deter my progress now.

We made a return trip to Seattle for the leg to be glued back together, laminated, and spray painted. We had to trust everything with the leg was the best they could do at that time. Home again, I started forcing myself to walk. There were tears of frustration, and I was exhausted. I was in pain because the muscles in my stump needed to get stronger. Pain, walk, pain, walk, that was my day. I was nervous about falling and my muscles were always tense to stabilize my balance, and walking gait. It didn't help that I relied only on a cane, refusing to use my crutches which I thought would draw more attention to my compromised mobility. The only way I was going to get stronger was to walk. Lack of muscle strength resulted in more pressure on the groin area, causing chafing and sores.

Through it all, I learned I am stronger than I ever thought.

Stretch More

Chapter 11

"Employment contributes to a person's ability to live independently, and everyone has a right to work. Our purpose is to empower people with disabilities to achieve a greater quality of life by obtaining and maintaining employment."

This was the mission statement of the agency that manages the rehabilitation program that made it possible for me to go to college.

Finally! Encouragement from an outside source to help me get on with my new life. As someone with only basic skills and no interests or qualifications for a job that would support me, the program was an opportunity to create an independent life. During the first two years at the junior college, I received fees for books, and while attending a four-year college to finish my teaching degree, I qualified for books and tuition.

With registration for classes set at Wenatchee Valley College, I was officially a college student. I needed to find a place to stay, even though the college was only thirty miles from my home. Driving back and forth was not something I needed to do, even though my parents made sure I had a safe car, a new 1966 red, Chevy II Nova. To meet my physical needs, this car was altered by moving the gas feed from right to left, as well as putting the dimmer switch on the console. It was one of the first cars in town to be customized for people with physical challenges.

First, I stayed with a friend of my mother with the stipulation I do chores for room and board. That lasted only a week. After coming home exhausted and hurting from a day walking all over campus, I was expected to stand over an ironing board. In addition, I didn't know I would be sharing not only the room but also the bed with another college girl that I had never met. I quickly decided to move out, but where?

We once again reached out to our community, and a high school classmate's grandmother, Esma, lived close to the college and agreed to let me stay during the week. On the weekends, I took my laundry and went home to be with my parents. Esma was a blessing. We had so much fun. The only issue we had was my boyfriend, Joe. She wasn't happy about him picking me up on his BSA motorcycle.

Skiing Uphill

Having no idea what to major in, I took the basic requirements for the first two years hoping something would grab my interest. I thought being a secretary was a possibility until I got to shorthand. Nope, not going there. While watching the Lloyd Bridges series, "Sea Hunt," on television, I thought I would become a diver. That was soon ruled out because I realized I didn't like getting water up my nose even when washing my face in the sink. Microbiology was next until I found it difficult to find anything in the microscope. Studying to be a doctor ended early in biology class when my lab partner had to dissect our frog. No,

I wasn't a good lab partner. So, I stuck with basic requirements. I started my last two years at Central Washington University in Ellensburg, Washington. This new campus presented challenges in maneuvering. Getting to one class required scaling down a bank and crossing a railroad track. Luckily, that was during summer school and there was no slippery snow to worry about.

Starting my junior year, I still didn't know what I was going to be when I grew up. In my last year of college, I found my love for teaching children. While taking a literature class, we went to the elementary school in town and read with students.

Skiing Uphill

I suddenly knew what I wanted to be... a teacher. I enrolled in education classes and found my passion. From then on, I was a four-point student on the Dean's list. Oh, I wish that high school counselor who told me not to go to college could see how successful I turned out to be! For the first time, I felt I was on my way to being a successful contributor to the community. That was the break I needed. Finally, my life started looking up.

Pat West Turner

College Graduate with parents, 1969

Small Idea, Big Rewards

Chapter 12

While I was completing my major in education in the late sixties, I received a gift from a literature professor that has traveled with me everywhere over the years. What started as a prize for answering a question continues to give me joy decades later. The reward was a crocheted bookworm with google eyes.

I came across this little critter while

unpacking boxes years later. Time had passed, and one day, there it was. It gave me the idea of making them for my classroom students to encourage them to study. My mother and grandma had taught me how to crochet when I was nine years old, so it

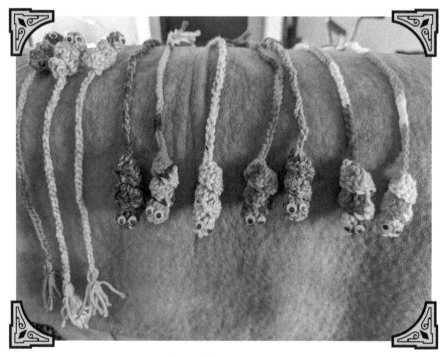

Bookworms

didn't take long to figure out how to repeat the stitches, and I've never stopped making them.

Being a teacher and always promoting literacy, my little bookworms became a very worthwhile tool to inspire students. It is amazing what children will do to earn a prize for academic recognition. The success of my students was always a primary goal, so I worked hard to instill in them the desire to learn. Some students took longer than others, but eventually, they reaped the rewards of working hard and got their bookworms. I laugh when I think back to the college professor who gave me mine.

When she dangled that bookworm in front of me, I so wanted it, not realizing that in the end, everyone got one. I wish I could tell her what an impact she made on my life.

To emphasize my passion for these worms, my husband was bored one day and counted all the worms that were stored in my cabinet which he called, the worm condominium. His count was a thousand, give or take a few. To date, they have traveled, zigzagging to twenty-seven parts of the world spanning from Iraq to Ukraine, Switzerland, Wales, Korea, Poland, and Peru to mention a few. They are great conversation starters, too. Coming back on the red-eye flight out of Kauai, I even met the pilot of our plane. After takeoff, he came out and thanked me for the gift one of the attendants took to him in the cockpit.

After eight years of teaching in California, I moved back to Washington to help my parents. I thought my career was over because of another tragic loss. This one was more emotional than losing my leg. Both of my parents were in ill health, my father with COPD (no, he never smoked), and my mother with a heart condition. Both had been in and out of the hospital often during the past five years. The last medical issues resulted in both being in the hospital a week apart. Dad was about ready to come home when I got the call at school that Mother had been admitted and placed on a respirator in ICU because of her breathing distress. Later tests showed her heart valve was leaking and performing at thirty percent. Later that day, I asked Joe to make calls to get a substitute teacher for my class while I cared for my parents.

Since my family was well known to the hospital staff, Dad was allowed to stay with my mother until the doctors determined if she would survive without the respirator. The answer became clear after a week, and she could not. Twelve hours after she was taken off of it, she passed.

The previous week, while keeping vigil in the hospital, followed by five days of planning for her service, I was physically and emotionally exhausted. I am thankful that years before we had gone to the funeral home and planned together the details of what she wanted.

Notices were made, the family gathered, and it was time for the service. We picked Dad up at the hospital and took him everywhere he needed to go during that day. Later, back in his room, he asked me, "What are we going to do?" I told him we were both tired and I would be back early the next day to figure things out. I knew he couldn't live by himself in the family home, fifteen miles away from me, so decisions needed to be talked about with the adult care staff for the best care to meet his needs. I kissed him goodnight and told him I loved him.

At seven o'clock the next morning, we got a phone call from the hospital. Dad had died. He had an enlarged heart because of years of lung issues. He was tired, and it gave out. What I think is, that after being married for fifty-two years, he had no reason to stay without his wife. Now I had another service to take care of. Being in shock, I did what needed to be done, and walked in a fog for the days before Dad's service.

The emotional toll this took on me was beyond the limits of comprehension. If it hadn't been for the LORD and my husband, Joe, I couldn't have survived. I felt the everlasting arms of Jesus preventing me from shooting in all directions like a spring released from its mounting. I cried until there were no more tears, then the tears came again, and again.

This all happened in the middle of October, not long after school had started. I took a couple of weeks leave and then returned on Halloween. That turned out to be too soon, as all I did that day was sit at my desk and cry as students were in and out. That afternoon I called the district office and said I needed a leave of absence. It was granted and I stayed home to grieve. Being their only child, and losing the identity of a daughter, I was coping with being an orphan.

For the remainder of the school year, I couldn't imagine going back. It was impossible to think or concentrate. I had until the end of the year to give my answer. Two reasons got me out of bed each day, the LORD who held me tight as I felt like I was going to implode, and Joe who held me when I sobbed, and let me be in my sorrow.

I continued seeing the hospital chaplain because he knew what I had been going through with my parents in the previous weeks. He asked me an interesting question: "Are you grieving?" "I think so, I'm sad and I cry." He sent me home with a task; "Write letters to both of your parents." When I started writing to Dad, it was like a light switch snapped on, and the tears came in torrents followed by gasping for breath. This didn't happen only once, but every time I started to write. What came out of the exercise; I was angry. Yes, initially

I was angry. All the time my mother was in ICU, I stayed close supporting him. I didn't know what we were going to do, and I knew how hard it would be watching Dad live without Mother. I was scared. It was gut-wrenching watching Dad stand up from his wheelchair to kiss Mom's forehead because the ugly, life-prolonging respirator was in her mouth. But I did, and I was there continuing to support him after she was gone. Now, I was all alone to grieve both. I felt like he had abandoned me, his beloved daughter.

Getting that thought on paper helped me process what I felt. As hard as it was to know that he was suddenly separated from his wife of fifty-two years, God saved me from that next step of caring for Dad alone. The funeral director summed it up, "Mary went ahead to get things ready for you, Ray."

The following spring, I went to help a teacher in her middle school classroom. After that day, with the emotional drain of continuous interactions, I knew I would not go back to teaching. About a year later, I realized I missed being with students and became a substitute teacher for the next fourteen years. What I liked was that if I didn't feel like going to school, I had flexibility.

When I started substitute teaching, the bookworms became part of my hook to encourage kids to focus. I waited until the last recess and then put the worms on a table so when they returned, they could see all the available colors. As they came through the door, their eyes would light up and they would ask "Do we get one?" Teasing, I would say, "No, I only wanted you to look at them." I'd laugh, then say "Yes, you each get one." That got them settled in their seats without delay. Then, there was the issue of who would get to choose first. The class helped with that decision. Before the last ten students came forward to choose, I added ten new worms as the colorful ones were always the first to go. The students who had already chosen a worm groaned when seeing the new colors. I told them when I was in school my last name started with "W" and I was always among the last to choose anything, so now I make sure those who are last still have a fair choice.

There is no end to where my little worms can travel. Now that I am retired, they go on trips and are freely shared. I met two women in Mexico on a zip line tour that ordered three hundred to take to Africa on a mission trip. Recently, I filled an order of 620 for a librarian who was retiring. She wanted to give a worm to every child in her elementary school. Worms even started showing up at random times in the 'lending library' at Pybus Public Market in Wenatchee, Washington.

It feels good when my gift is received. I love to see the surprised look on people's faces, followed by smiles when I share something so little, colorful, and useful with strangers. Quite often they say they will pass the worm on to a child or grandchild at home. When they are sharing the joy, I always have them take one for themselves, too. I've made many new friends this way. I am leaving a memorable imprint from my part of the world, especially when I give them away while I'm traveling. I feel like a friendship ambassador sharing a gift from my part of the world. The message at the bottom of my business card reads, "Goal: Educate, encourage, and inhabit the world with 'worms' and smiles."

Two years ago, I picked up another hobby, painting "kindness" rocks. I started watercolor painting after I retired from teaching but struggled with the dreaded need to be perfect. A rock isn't as intimidating as a canvas. With rock, I paint over what I don't like and paint something different. Again, the purpose of this movement is to bring joy to the person who finds it. The idea is to drop painted rocks in a space close to where people walk. I drop the happy little stones at grocery or art stores, some are in the gravel in front of our home, and other stones find their way into clothing stores or outside of clinics.

The Saturday before Valentine's Day, it was snowing. So, I took my rocks inside our public market and handed them out randomly. One lady got tears in her eyes and said, "You don't know how much I needed this today." Others appreciated the gesture of unsolicited kindness. I love to see people smile.

Jokester on a Limb

Chapter 13

Children are inquisitive, especially the little ones. They pop out with a question to a parent. "Why does she have only one leg?" This is especially true when I'm using my wheelchair. But when I wore a prosthesis and had shorts or a short dress on, they picked out the different-looking knee right away. When I see them watching me, I know that an inquiry is going to happen. I will stop and ask the parent, "Do you have a minute? I would like to tell them what happened." They do, and as soon as I tell them what happened, their curiosity turns to understanding. I gear my story to be age-appropriate, and even then, they may not process it all, but the next handicapped person they see might not be so scary. If I weren't an amputee, I wouldn't be credible. Plus, now I have a chance to talk about challenges and the importance of staying strong and not giving up. I am grateful to have the gift to teach people from all walks of life...young and old.

The following snippets come from

funny encounters I've experienced over the years. I have worked hard not to be defined because I have one leg. Most of these stories are a compliment to me as it demonstrates that people do forget I have one leg.

* * * * *

While substitute teaching a kindergarten class, I had on a long dress. I was not wearing my prosthesis that day because of a sore at the top of the socket, and it was too painful to wear. The children were almost standing on their heads trying to look up my dress. I kept assuring them I had only one leg. They believed there had to be another foot. Finally, one asked me, "Where is your shoe?"

* * * * *

Joe, my Golf Pro husband, was talking about the importance of balance while swinging a golf club. To explain what he meant he gave examples of drills he used. In all seriousness, he asked me if I knew how hard it is to balance on one leg! "Ah, yes, Honey, and that question is going viral!"

* * * * *

I was having dinner with a group of

friends. As usual, the men were sitting at one end of the table talking about golfing, skiing, and biking, while the women were at the other talking about hair, nails, and pedicures. A friend turned to me and asked if I had ever had a pedicure. I told her "No, but I had talked to my nail guy, and he said I could have it for half price." Without taking a breath, she asked, "Well, how come"? I looked at her without saying a word. When the realization showed in her eyes, I held up my hands in surrender and said, "I am sorry, I am soooooooooooo sorry!"

* * * * *

At one point I dated an amputee who was also a three-track snow skier. We are described that way as we leave three tracks in the snow, one ski, and two outriggers. Outriggers are orthopedic, armband crutches mounted on short ski tips used for balance. I will talk about this more in chapter 15. Traveling to races, we had four skis in the rack on top of the car. This was not unusual, but all were different models! Going through towns we got some very strange looks.

Northwest Ski Instructor

AUTUMN
1968
VOL. 2 NO. 3

Official Journal of The Pacific Northwest Ski Instructors Association

*Pat and Jerry at White Pass
wowing the crowd*

Pat West Turner

* * * * *

When teaching school in Placerville, California, I volunteered with an amputee ski group on weekends. When we went inside the lodge to eat, it was fun being the last one to leave to watch the expressions on the faces of the unsuspecting skiers. Amputee skiing was a new sport in the late sixties and there were only a few us out there, especially women.

* * * * *

I remember shopping in Seattle with a college friend. We had dates but didn't have time to shower and eat before going out, so we ordered room service. When the gentleman brought our dinner, walked in the door, and saw my foot and part of a leg sticking out from under wadded tissue paper and open boxes, he got so flustered he sat the tray on the floor by the door and left. Later, we paid for dinner at the front desk. Yes, we staged that scene.

* * * * *

Driving home from the same outing we stopped for gas. Remember the days when the attendant pumped gas AND washed the windows? As the attendant was washing the back window and realized a leg and foot were sticking out from under a pile of boxes, I can only imagine what he thought! As his brain was processing what he was seeing, he almost rubbed a hole through the window.

* * * * *

Waiting in line for a table at a restaurant, a couple of young boys were watching with curiosity. Finally, I asked if they wanted to know what happened. "I bet it was a shark!" one boy said. After I laughed, I said, "Yeah, a shark in the shape of a car."

Skiing Uphill

* * * * *

The first few days of college, on my prostheses, I didn't use my cane when walking with my boyfriend because I always held onto his arm. One afternoon we walked to the library together then he continued to football practice. I watched him walk away, but when I turned to go inside, I realized no cane or arm. First was panic, but next, I had decisions to make. I could call after him or remain in the same spot and stand there for at least an hour until he came back, or I walk on into the library. The best confidence-building action

I made was to walk into the library without an aide. After that day, the cane stayed home.

* * * * *

Boys I graduated with from high school were also at the same college. They thought it great fun to play with my prosthesis. Sitting in the commons, one would attract my attention in one direction while the boy sitting next to me would run a finger up and down my knee. It didn't take long to catch on because of the amusing looks I was getting.

Unlikely Encounter

Chapter 14

Joe, my husband, was aware of me long before I knew he existed. The first time he saw me, I was learning to three-track snow ski at Mission Ridge, Wenatchee's local ski area. He turned to his friend and announced, "I'm going to marry that girl." That answered my earlier question about what I was thinking while in the hospital, *"Will anyone find a one-legged person attractive?"* I wouldn't get that answered until years later.

I was slowly and deliberately making my way down the beginner's slope. My ski instructor constantly reminded me to breathe. I was concentrating so hard and holding my breath that it weakened my muscles due to a lack of oxygen. He solved that by training me to breathe every time I made a turn, which was quite often. It was amazing how that made a difference, my leg felt stronger, and I wasn't gasping for breath anymore.

A couple of weeks later, Joe saw me in a bowling class at the local junior college where we enrolled right out of high school. Being the "shy guy," he professed to be, I wasn't aware of him even then. He eventually worked up the courage to ask me out. It wasn't until later he told me what he heard at a party. A young man I had broken up with the previous week was in attendance and he wasn't happy about the split. He told the guys they should ask me out because I was easy. Joe asked me for a date and discovered I wasn't so easy.

Joe and I dated for about a year and a half, enjoying the college scene and having fun getting to know each other. From the start, we knew he was destined for Viet

Pat West Turner

Pat and Joe, Homecoming,
Wenatchee Valley College

Nam. Without telling me, he enlisted, knowing that if he didn't, he would be drafted. The advantage of joining up was he had the choice of specialties that interested him, instead of automatically having to carry a gun. He chose culinary school. That didn't get him out of basic training, but his future looked more promising.

I wanted to get married before he left, but he wouldn't because of the stories he heard from friends who left a new wife at home while serving their country. He didn't want to put me through the fear each day of not knowing if he was okay, and the loneliness of being separated. His thinking and concern for me were beyond his years, and for that, I am, eternally grateful. I didn't want to wait, all the time thinking he didn't love me, so I broke up with him weeks before he left for basic training. Here's the amazing part, ten years later we got back together and married.

During the ten years we were apart, I moved on with my life. After completing two years at junior college, I went to Central Washington University to complete my teaching degree. After earning a BA in Special Education, I married and moved to northern California for my first job. During the eight years I lived in Folsom, commuting fifty miles round trip to Placerville, I finished my fifth-year requirements and got a second major in Social Sciences to update my teaching certificate for California. After eight years of teaching, I returned home, single.

How did I get to California? To finish my degree on time, I went to summer school to take a couple more required credits. One of my instructors was from California. At the end of his class, he told me if I needed a job to call him. After several applications were rejected in Washington because of an overabundance of teachers, I called him. My first husband and I filled a U-Haul truck with our meager possessions and were off to California.

We were on an adventure moving out of the only state in which I had ever lived. Oh, and what a welcome we got arriving in the Sacramento Valley in the heat of August. The air was hard to breathe, and the smog made it more oppressive. Fast forward to the beginning of fall. I was excited for the cooler temperatures and rain soon to follow, like at home, but that was not to be. The field I drove through to get to the freeway smelled like a wet dog for at least two weeks, following that first welcomed rain. The heat had killed all the enzymes in the grass, which took time to re-develop. Another, not so "welcome to California." The marriage did not work out.

I gave myself a divorce present of a month-long trip to New Zealand to ski with amputee skiers at Mt. Hutt. I had been corresponding with an attorney from New Zealand who was an advocate for handicap rights. We became acquainted through the Mt. Hood Flying Outrigger Ski Club.

When I started skiing, my instructor from Mission Ridge, Otto Ross, got the outriggers for me from the Flying Outrigger Ski Club, located at Mt. Hood, OR. Plus, when I started participating in some of the

Pat West Turner

Pat and Ski Instructor, Otto Ross

Mt. Hood downhill ski races and members of the organization got to know me, they knew I could provide more insights for the New Zealand attorney about the challenges of being an amputee. They gave me his address and we started corresponding. This was years before computers, and yet, he wrote two to three-page, legal-length letters regularly. Ready for another adventure, I set my sights on visiting New Zealand. He was delighted when I told him I wanted to visit, and please arrange families for me to stay with. I flew by myself for about six hours from Sacramento to Los Angeles, and another thirteen hours from there to

Auckland, New Zealand. While visiting I traveled on both the North and South Islands, partly by train and the rest by car with the families with whom I stayed.

New Zealand is a beautiful part of the world, offering many opportunities for recreation and activities. I arrived in June, after school was out, which was their winter. The terrain was comprised of lowlands or mountains. When skiing there was snow but when traveling around the roads were clear and easy to maneuver.

One of the towns on the North Island was Rotorua. It is renowned for its geothermal activities and is rich in Māori culture. My friend joined me for a short horseback ride, nine holes of golf, followed by a dip in the geothermal pool. The interesting thing about the golf course, there was a short electric fence around the greens to keep grazing sheep in the fairway. I can't say enough about the hospitality I received the entire time I was there.

Another area I stopped in was Mt. Ruapehu where I stayed at the Chateau Tongariro. After a morning of skiing, I returned to the lowlands on their mountain transport called the Goat. This vehicle had wooden bench seats with no cushions and minimal heat. There were windows and

I chose to look straight out over the valley instead of focusing on the steep bank beside us. While I was in New Zealand, I went skiing with a group of two-legged skiers. One of my new friends entered me in a ski race called NZSTAR. It had the same format as our NASTAR that we had in the United States. NASTAR is an acronym for NAtional STAndard Race, which is the world's largest known recreational ski and snowboard race program. It allows ski or snowboard racers of all ages and abilities, through a handicapping system to compare themselves with one another and with the national champions, regardless of when and where the race is held. Many U.S. Ski Team stars got their start ski racing in NASTAR programs. When I won a silver medal, the news traveled over the AP wire media, and the sports editor from my town, Dick Piper, picked it up. He followed my skiing progress after losing my leg, mainly because I started skiing within a year of my accident. He called my parents and said he

7-19-7?

New Zealand

Powder Hound Magazine
(Pat wins a silver medal)

wanted to see me when I got home from my trip. I called him and he wrote a follow-up article with a photo of me.

A friend told Joe I was single again so when he saw the story in the paper, he called me and asked me to dinner. At that time, Joe had bought into a small logging company. The night of our first date he was an hour late picking me up in his work truck because he had worked later than usual. He called to say he was running late. When he arrived his two big black labrador dogs were in the back as well as his logging equipment. We waited an hour for a table at the restaurant. While we waited, we talked about our jobs, what it's like living in California, and about my plans to move back to Washington. After dinner we went promptly to the service station for gas and oil for his chain saws, then he took me home, kissed me good night, and left. Watching him leave, I thought, "Hum, that was interesting." It didn't seem like an effective way to "rekindle" a former relationship fire!

I returned to California to finish my eighth year of teaching with plans to move back to my hometown of Entiat in June as both of my parents were not in good health and I needed to be closer to home. Before Thanksgiving, Joe called and chatted for about half an hour while my California boyfriend was sitting in the living room. We hung up and again I thought, "Hum, that was interesting." Later, he told me he called to ask if I would fly home for the Thanksgiving vacation if he sent me the money. He was afraid I would say "no," so he didn't ask. I guess it's true, he is shy.

At Christmas, I was excited to be with my family as well as to make final plans for my move home. On that first day home for a two-week break from school, Joe called and asked me to dinner. That first night, after seeing him only one time in ten years he asked me to marry him. WHAT!?! For at least the last three of the eight years of my previous marriage, it was miserable. I certainly didn't want to jump into another after having had my freedom for only two years, and I had a boyfriend in California. My first response was, "Really? You don't even know who I am after ten years of being apart. No, I am weird right now, and need time to figure out who I am and what I am looking for in a relationship." He tried to convince me we were meant to be together, and that he loved me by telling me, "From the time we broke up, all my girlfriends knew about you." Oh, that's a new line, and not reassuring. What I later learned was this 'shy guy' was dating four girls at the time he was thinking about asking me out. There's another red flag!

Joe wined and dined me every night I was home and every night for two weeks he asked me the same question, with the same reasoning: "Will you marry me? I love you and we are meant to be together." "No, no, and no!"

Joe was logging in December, even in the snow. When he went up the valley to work, miles from my home, the equipment had frozen during the night. On the way back home, he stopped by for one more try. We were sitting on the floor in the living room when he asked the same question with the same reasoning. My response wasn't romantic, but I finally said, "YES, okay, now get off my back!" He was quite satisfied with himself, as he gave me that, 'I won' smile. We agreed we wouldn't tell anyone that we were engaged until I moved back in June. Oh, and there was my current boyfriend in California, oh boy. He agreed and went on his merry way home to clean up and then come back for dinner with my parents and me. The next day I had to leave in the dark hours of the morning for Seattle to catch my plane to Sacramento.

The reason I didn't want to say anything

is that both of us would have some explaining to do with both sets of parents, especially our mothers. His mother was not happy with me because I broke her son's heart by breaking up with him ten years earlier before he left for Viet Nam. My mother was not happy with him for what happened at the local park, years earlier. We were walking up a slight incline and Joe popped me on the behind and told me to hurry up, right in front of my mother. At least we were starting on an even playing field, my mom didn't like Joe and his mom wasn't fond of me.

Joe arrived for dinner, and I greeted

him at the door. He had a brightly wrapped Christmas gift for me. He told me to wait until I was on the plane to open it. He knew better than that as I began to quickly tear off the paper. My mother was standing there and when I took the top off, I realized I was looking at a little black box, and inside, yup, there was an engagement ring. The first thing Mother said was "You better go tell your father!"

"Joe, what happened to our secret?" It's no secret anymore as he had already told his mother. Her first words were, "Remember what she did to you before?" We both love our mothers dearly and understood their concerns. Out of love for their children, they were still trying to protect us from being hurt, even when we were thirty-something years old.

Joe and I agree that had we married when we were so young, it probably would not have lasted. The first few years we were married were rough. I carried baggage from the first marriage that Joe helped me put down. He pushed buttons that brought up memories of hard times. He was patient and reminded me when I got mad that he wasn't my first husband. When I settled down, I couldn't resist the opportunity to remind him, "I tried to warn you!" Even

Honeymoon in Tahiti, 1979

after years of marriage, we are still figuring things out. We both agree that loving each other is a given, but still liking each other is a blessing. What I know, for sure, is I have a husband who loves me to my very core, and I love him back!

Freedom on the Mountain

Chapter 15

The winter after I lost my leg, 1966, the ski season was about to start at the newly developed Mission Ridge ski area, located about thirty minutes out of Wenatchee. Otto started instructing for the ski school. Before the season started, he approached my parents and asked if they thought I wanted to ski again. Not knowing the answer, they told him to ask me. I don't remember hesitating a moment before I said, "Sure." He contacted the Flying Outrigger Ski Club located on Mt. Hood in Oregon for assistance in teaching an amputee. They sent a manual and the needed equipment called outriggers. These consisted of armband crutches mounted on short ski tips to aid in balance. With the manual zipped in Otto's jacket, a single ski clamped to my ski boot, and outriggers hooked to my arms, we headed to the rope tow. It wasn't long before I fell. As Otto was getting the manual out of his ski jacket, I figured out the logical way of getting up. Back on my ski, he teasingly said, "Get back down there, I haven't told you how to get up." After falling and getting back up over, and over again during the first-hour session, I was out of breath and exhausted, but the exercise increased my stamina quickly. The amazing thing was I wasn't yet walking on my prosthesis. They were back-to-back learning challenges.

Once I stayed upright, my immediate goal was to progress from the rope tow to the chair lift. It was tricky being pulled up the slope with the rope tow. First, I had to inch up to the flat loading area, get my ski turned to point uphill, balance, then move both outriggers to one hand, slowly grab the moving rope with my gloved hand, while maintaining my balance, and with luck, away I went. When it came time to get off at the landing, I balanced while turning my ski, transferred the second outrigger from my right hand to my left, and clamped the armband back on my arm. I was ready to point my ski downhill to gain enough momentum to make a turn or two. Gliding down that little hill, I felt the wind on my face for the first time since I lost my leg, and I was moving freely. I repeated this on the rope every Saturday for a couple of months. Finally, I could turn both ways, side slip, stop on command, and walk uphill using the edges of my outriggers, meeting all the requirements for advancing to the chair lift. The first time I sat on the chair I had no idea of the new skills I was yet to learn.

With every success came challenges. After I felt comfortable on chair one, it was time for chair two, and the top of the mountain. Mission was a new ski area with one rope tow and two chair lifts, so my choice of runs was limited. This advancement to chair two turned out to be premature. The steeper and narrower runs challenged my newly acquired skills. I had to turn whether I was ready or not. Falling multiple times, it took four hours from the top of the mountain to the bottom! The muscles in my leg felt like they were on fire.

By the time I reached the top of chair one, I was, again, out of breath and exhausted as I had been during the first lesson on the rope tow. The terrain was familiar, but I still had a distance to go before reaching the comfort of the lodge and a warm fire. The only way I could rest my leg was by sitting on the snow. But to get back up was no easy task and added to my fatigue.

Once again, Otto came to my rescue. He bent from the waist and let me bend over his flat back to take some pressure off my leg and arms. When rested, I got my outriggers hooked back on my arms, then I was off again. Nothing looked sweeter than the last corner before seeing the lodge. I made it! Did I give up after that? No, I worked even harder to master skiing so I could visit the upper slopes again. At the end of the season, after more hours on chair one, I made that same four-hour run from top to midway in eight minutes.

I became a much better skier on one ski than I ever was on two. Within the year, I was going to the top of the mountain and keeping up with the best of them.

The next winter, I worked for Mission Ridge as an instructor while I finished my

Pat West Turner

Pat at top of Mission Ridge

second year of junior college in Wenatchee.

You are wondering how I could instruct people with two legs. We had a cadet training program for high school students to become instructors. The ones who were the most skilled skiers skied with me to demonstrate the turns I wanted my students to learn. I still see people around town who remind me I was their instructor and tell me how I had influenced their lives, not only in skiing but also in demonstrating there is nothing you can't do if you want it bad enough.

I particularly remember a class of six fourth-grade boys. The lesson for the day was skiing moguls. The place to practice the skills was Hot Dog Hill. Standing at the top, I reviewed what they needed to do, including the best place on the mogul to turn, and how to keep their speed under control. Before I finished talking, one of the boys took off. Of course, his friends followed him instead of waiting for the demonstration my helper was about to do. Now I had a field of moguls littered with bodies. In the ski world, that's called "a yard sale." Everyone had fallen leaving goggles, ski poles, and skis all over the hill. When they finally got all their equipment on, and we gathered at the bottom, I said, "Now, are you ready to listen?" Sheepishly they nodded, and we slid down to the chair landing to go up and try it again. They turned out to be a fun group. I got their total attention the day I demonstrated a 360-degree turn. I was telling them what I wanted to happen, then my cadet demonstrated. They thought it would be fun for ME to do one, too. Well, okay, why not? My turn wasn't pretty or perfect, but I made a jerky 360-degree turn. They showed their appreciation for my effort by applauding me. From that day on, I think they would have followed me off a cliff. I didn't expect them to be perfect and what better way to demonstrate than to put myself out there and not be perfect?

During the year of instructing, I also participated in slalom racing on Mt. Hood. Since three-track skiing was new, there were few women competitors, so I raced against men in the same ability class. After my first year of racing, there was a skier I looked forward to seeing at the next race. He came with his so-called trainer. When they discovered he was racing in the same ability class as me, they skied off and left me by myself on the mountain to finish shadowing the course by myself. The only reason I can think for them to do that is they didn't want to give me an advantage by allowing me to tag along. We raced: I won first place. My dad took a picture of him getting his second-place trophy and me getting my first-place trophy. When I had the film developed, I promptly mailed him both photos.

I continued to ski while teaching in Placerville, California. I worked with a group of amputee skiers and was privileged to instruct a veteran who had lost an arm and his opposite leg in Viet Nam. He was an inspiration to me. I needed to tell him what I wanted him to do while we were riding up the lift, because as soon as his ski hit the snow he was gone, and I had to keep

Pat West Turner

Pat accepting lst place trophy from Gretchen
Fraser, the first American
woman to win a Gold Medal in
1948 Winter Olympics

up with him.

There were many experiences I would have missed if I had two legs, When I skied with the amputee group at Mt. Hood in Oregon, their group asked me to be on the United States amputee demonstration team for an international ski event, 8th INTERSKI, held in 1968 in Aspen, Colorado. What a thrill for a nineteen-year-old to have a two-week, paid vacation in Aspen.

This one sport opened many doors throughout my life. Over the years, I have been an encouragement to anyone who saw me ski. Many times, people approached me to say, "If you can do this, so can I." I am

INTERSKI

8. INTERSKI
1968 ASPEN

PATRICIA WEST

U.S.S.A

DEMONSTRATION TEAM

PAT WEST INVITED TO 8TH INTERSKI

Amputee skier Pat West of Entiat has been invited to participate in the 8th Interski at Aspen, Colo.

Miss West and seven other amputee skiers from the Far West will demonstrate their single-ski technique for the benefit of the world's best ski technicians at Aspen April 25. Miss West was the only woman selected for the team.

The Wenatchee Valley College coed, although skiing on a single ski for only two seasons, entered two races this winter and was victorious in her division both times. One of those races was the National Amputee Skiing Championships.

The 8th Interski brings together the top ski technicians in the world in a 10-day symposium starting April 19.

Headline of newspaper article

grateful I took the challenge of learning to ski on one leg.

Even back at Mission Ridge, I was always ready for a challenge, I began switching from outriggers to regular ski poles. As my balance increased, my technique improved. I practiced on the lower slopes, but one day, when I was higher up on the mountain, one of my outriggers broke. With the help of the ski patrol, I got the message to Joe to bring me a spare set. I didn't want to wait as I thought it was okay and borrowed my Aunt Virginia's ski poles. I was thinking I'd take it easy.

Cautiously, I made the first turn in the

soft spring snow. At the beginning of the first turn, my edge carved deep into the snow and I crashed. When I fell, the side of my stump hit first. Then my pole became trapped under my ski forcing my left shoulder to plow through the snow until I stopped sliding. Face down, bellowing like a wounded animal, I couldn't move.

Seconds later, the urgent call blasted over the Mission Ridge Ski Patrollers' walkie-talkies, "Pat's down, everyone come, above Toketie split, NOW!" Within minutes, help arrived. I hurt so badly I couldn't cry but continued making guttural howls. Joe and I had recently finished a first aid refresher course where the instructor said more people die from shock than injuries. I was in so much pain that I knew I was going to die.

Joe, also a ski instructor at Mission Ridge, was contacted regarding my location and told that I needed an outrigger, as mine had broken. He was riding on the chair with another outrigger when he saw several ski patrollers attending a skier on the snow. When he saw my red jacket and outriggers, he knew it was me.

Stabilizing my stump and shoulder, the patrollers turned me over and attempted to place me in the toboggan. With all the splints and wraps I wouldn't fit below the sides. This was necessary to have securely strapped me in for the ride off the mountain. To remedy this, they all placed their fanny packs with various first aid items on the bottom of the sled. That lifted me high enough and now they were able to secure me with straps. I was ready for the descent off the mountain.

Waiting for the ambulance, I was transferred from the sled onto a cot in the patrol room. While lying there I tried to rub my shoulder with my hand to make the ache feel better. Then I realized why it hurt, it was dislocated because four fingers fell in the curve of the socket, not on the top of my shoulder.

At the hospital, the diagnosis in the emergency room was that I had a dislocated shoulder plus a broken femur an inch below my hip on the stump side. Unfortunately, they could not cast my stump, so the surgery required to set the bone in place included a titanium plate anchored in by a screw in the hip, which in turn was fastened with four screws longer than you hang a door!

It took months to recover. There were complications later as the femur had not been set straight, and I lost stabilizing muscles required for balance when I started

Pat West Turner

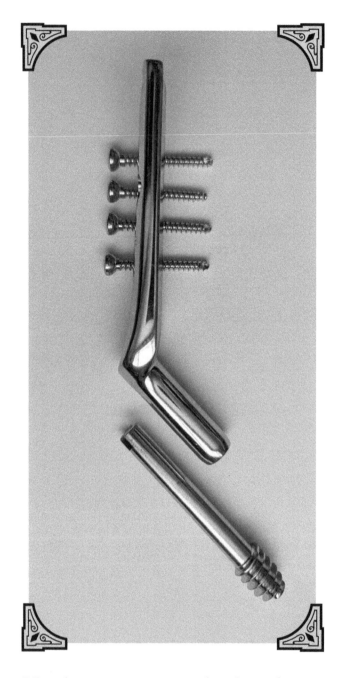

Hardware to secure broken femur

walking with my new prosthesis. The next season I recovered enough from my injuries and regardless of my confidence being bruised, I returned to skiing. Two years later, on the first day of the season, I crashed on what we call death cookies. These are chunks of ice formed when the snow freezes. The fall broke my pelvic bone on the stump side.

Only then did the doctors realize I have severe osteoporosis for lack of weight-bearing on the bone. That was another emotional blow. Over the years, I had become a strong walker and now the doctors were telling me that didn't matter!

They were right. When I pulled my stump into the socket, stability happened only through tissue containment. There was never any weight-bearing on the bone as the end of the stump was too sensitive for any kind of pressure.

It was hard enough losing the ability to walk the first time. Now because of the misaligned bone, I wasn't even back to square one. Frustration and the fear of falling took over. The sport I loved since I was five years old, now scared me. In the final year, I skied alone. I didn't want people to see me cry as I rode to the top of chair one, skied down, got on the lift again, and cried some more. Fear of injury was so strong I quit torturing myself and permitted myself to stop skiing. The end of my skiing career was a long-drawn-out, painful decision.

Why is the desire to ski so strong in my core? I enjoyed this sport for over 30 years without injury and now this. "Okay, mountain, I know it's not your fault, but you continue to look so enticing." I hate to let this freedom go, but I must. My heart wants to come back, but for once my common-sense screams, "NO!"

Discovering New Adventures

Chapter 16

After I lost my leg, a friend offered to teach me to water ski. The nearest water was, at the time, officially called Rocky Reach Reservoir, formed above Rocky Reach Dam, one of the hydroelectric power dams built on the Columbia River in 1961. Because the reservoir covered the entire town of Entiat, the community held several meetings with the PUD asking to officially change the name to Lake Entiat, and eventually, they agreed.

Taking up this challenge was more painful than snow skiing. I thought after all the exercise I had during the winter, I was strong, but that was not the case. Pulled behind a boat found a new set of unused muscles. This sport takes an incredible amount of strength in the core, plus arms, back, and shoulders, and water is not soft when falling. I attempted starting in deep water, sitting on a dock, sitting in a lawn chair with water up to my arms, and sitting on a friend's knee. When I was successful, I realized it was all up to me. The day I got the timing right, using the pull of the boat, and pushing myself into a standing position, suddenly I was up! I didn't go far, but I was up. Finally, success! Before long I was comfortable crossing the wake, as well as hanging on when the boat was traveling in a wide circle, and I was being whipped around at what seemed like warp speed. Sure, it looks easy when watching someone zig-zag back and forth behind a boat, but here again, we run into problems because of our weight distribution. I learned to attack the wake with my weight on the back of the ski to keep the tip from catching on the crest of the wake.

In the beginning, I was making somewhat ungraceful three-point landings when coming back to shore but quickly learned to judge my speed and the distance I had in which to land. When the distance was right, I'd give a gentle pull on the rope, releasing it and with arms extended, slowly settle into the water. This gave me the feeling of balancing on one leg. After my ski reached the bottom, I would pull my foot from the ski with a slight hop and remain standing on the bottom. Then, with ski in hand, I was ready to hop back to shore.

I was often stiff, sore, sunburned, and water-logged just to mention a few of the

Pat with slalom waterski

inconveniences, but looking back, I can honestly say it was worth it.

One time when I lost control and crashed, I lost a gold nugget earring, dislocated my thumb, and the bottom of my two-piece suit ended around my thigh. Luckily, I put myself back together while waiting for the boat to return. Not until I pulled myself over the side of the railing did, I realize my top wasn't exactly covering me, which was a bit awkward since my dad was in the boat along with other guy friends.

When I lived in California, I had the opportunity to waterski at least three days a week on the American River near

Skiing Uphill

Sacramento. I became confident enough that I bought a Short Swing waterski. Skiing on a river is different than a lake. For one thing, the wake made by the boat dissipates faster than on a lake partly because of the river's current. On a lake, the wake hits the shore, then ripples back, causing cross-waves. I prefer the smoother river. Like snow skiing, the feeling of the wind on my face and the freedom of movement will always be a thrill. Again, I turned heads when people saw an amputee cutting through the water. Like snow skiing, I didn't meet another woman in the sport.

I waterskied for the last time above Rocky

Reach Dam. Cutting through the wake, I hit a piece of driftwood and bounced over the water like a skipping stone! I didn't lose anything, but it felt like I hit the pavement in the parking lot. Another door closed.

Was that incident an end to my active participation in sports? No! Riding a tandem bicycle with my husband was another activity we enjoyed for years. This is not a sport for everyone. Two people riding on one bike takes incredible communication and trust.

The captain, Joe, is in the front where he steers, shifts, brakes, avoids bumps, controls speed (occasionally requiring a thump on the head to slow down), communicates direction, and most helpful, pedals. The back-seat position, the stoker, me, was a bit more flexible. My responsibilities were to pedal, and not anticipate what direction my captain is going to turn by prematurely leaning. When approaching an obstacle, I looked in the middle of Joe's back to keep from favoring one way or the other by shifting my weight. I was also the snack and water bar. Another plus of being a touch away from Joe is that I have a captive audience.

Our favorite time to ride was early in the morning on the loop trail that runs beside the Columbia River. Before the sun comes up the Columbia River is as smooth as glass, osprey are catching fish to feed their young, rabbits dash across the trail, and the air is crisp and smells fresh. The Apple Capital Loop Trail for bikers and walkers was completed in 1994, spanning ten miles of asphalt surfaces. Later, the trail expanded beyond the loop to cover approximately twenty-five miles.

Trust is the main component of tandem riding. When Joe takes the bike in to be checked each fall, the only reminder he gives the technician is, "Do what you need to do, remember, Pat's on the back."

Skiing Uphill

This activity has also gone by the wayside. I'm spending more time in a wheelchair for safety after several falls while using crutches. I can no longer tolerate the little bike seat.

Joe and Pat In Tandem

One of the hardest falls I took was at my birthday party at a friend's house, who also shares the same birth date. Joe and I had just arrived when I stopped to talk with a friend in the kitchen. Turning, not realizing snow had melted from my crutches onto the linoleum, I started to move, and the crutch slipped out from under me. I landed headfirst on the heated surface. It happened so fast I didn't have time to take my hands off the grips. Blood gushed everywhere as I severed my temporal artery. With luck, there were two nurses and an EMT at the party. A friend sat beside me and kept pressure on my wound with towels until the ambulance arrived, and off to the hospital I went.

There is a successful conclusion to this disaster. Well, yes, I lived to talk about it, that's a good thing, but there's more. Many scans were taken of my head and neck. The one on my head showed a concussion, and the one on my neck revealed I had thyroid cancer.

With the diagnosis from the ultra-scan more tests needed to be run for specific information on the extent of affected lymph nodes, and what kind of cancer. Within the week I was scheduled to have biopsies of the nodes in my neck. I shouldn't have looked at the needle lying on the steel tray, but I did. At the thought of that long needle going into my neck, sweat beaded up on my forehead. I can truthfully say it wasn't as bad as I expected. Sure, there was a poke and a sting, but it was quick.

The next day I received a call from the endocrinologist's nurse asking if I could come in that afternoon. Initially, I knew this was not good news, as I had only had the procedure the day before. Sitting in the room waiting for the doctor, I hoped against hope that the news wasn't what I expected. After hearing the words, "it is cancer," I don't remember why she excused herself and said she would be right back. I looked at Joe, tears welling up and feeling like I had been hit in the stomach, I said, "I don't want this. No, I don't want this." After processing what had happened, the tears flowed and Joe held me while I cried. The doctor returned and said surgery would be scheduled soon. I asked how soon. Then, she asked if we had a vacation planned. "Yes, we are scheduled to go to Kauai for two weeks." She assured me the type of cancer I had was not aggressive and the surgery could be scheduled for when we returned. With that reassurance, we left for vacation, and I didn't dwell on the fact my neck would be cut open when we got home.

Two days after we returned, I went in for surgery. I had to stay overnight as the entire thyroid was removed, and both sides had visible cancer cells. Outside of a sore throat, recovery was quick. It made me nervous when the surgeon said he took more time looking for what he didn't want to cut than what he needed to cut. The only treatment after the removal was one radioactive iodine treatment that was supposed to kill any lingering cells.

Six months later the ultra-scan picked up more suspicious lymph nodes. I went back in for another biopsy, and yes, it needed to come out. Back into surgery, but this time the node was right next to my voice box. Initially, the surgeon didn't know if it had attached to the voice box or not. If it had, I would come out with no voice. Trusting God, I knew that wasn't going to happen. The surgeon said he picked it up with forceps and lopped it off. The ultra-scan I had six months later was clear and I have been clear for fourteen years, with no other occurrence of cancer in my body.

They say there is something good that comes out of everything. If I hadn't fallen when I did, they wouldn't have found cancer. Yes, I'm a believer in this statement, because good things have happened to me following all the mishaps since losing my leg.

Now, it was time to find something else Joe and I can do together. Thanks to a friend we acted. One night our pinochle group met for the monthly dinner and cards. During dessert, our friend suggested we form girl and guy bowling teams to participate in the yearly fundraiser for CASA, for which she is a volunteer. Her responsibility is to work with legal and child welfare professionals and service providers to ensure that the judge has all the information needed to make the most well-informed decisions for each child.

Skiing Uphill

My first thought about what she was suggesting was, "Really"! The more we talked, the more I became intrigued, and said "Why not, but under one condition, we all bowl from a wheelchair." With that in place, we started planning for that day at the event. First, we needed a name, and the Chair Chicks were ready to roll.

We gathered at the bowling alley to figure out how to make this work. Everyone was on an even learning curve and that was entertaining. I provided an extra wheelchair, and the fun began. In the first game, I used bumpers. It became evident that without them every throw would have been a gutter ball. Knowing at the event, I couldn't use the bumpers I had to figure it out as I did when I got up on the water and snow skis when I first was learning both sports.

The challenge was leaning out far enough from the big wheel, so I didn't bounce off the metal when I swung the ball. Learning was trial and error softened by much laughter. The day came and our team stood out like I always did, but mainly because of the fun we were having.

In the end, our scores didn't matter as it was all about raising money through pledges for the kids and having fun while doing it. Our team placed third for raising the most money and for a year the team members took turns receiving the prize of a monthly bouquet of flowers.

For the gift of confidence, a friend including me in doing something new, I am grateful. A new sport was born for Joe and me. It didn't take long to get serious about this new adventure. Joe purchased bowling shoes. We both picked out a ball, and I got, what I call, my bowling chair. I no longer have the big wheel to deal with because I have a transport chair. The one drawback is I have a difficult time getting around since I'm unable to move without the big wheel.

I can move it a little with my foot if I don't have far to go. When it's my turn at the line, Joe pushes me up, then pulls me back. I remind him this is the only time it's okay to push me around.

After a year or more of trial and error, we joined a winter bowling league and became a part of a new family of bowlers. With the love and encouragement from my husband and other bowlers, I excelled from a score of 34 the first time without bumpers to an average of 102 by the end of the winter league. Reinventing myself yet another time was worth the effort. I, once again, demonstrated I am always up for a challenge. Recently, in preparation for this winter league, I bowled my best game ever in the wheelchair, 155! No, that is not what I want my handicap to be based on each week.

Pushing the Limits

Chapter 17

My fascination with up-in-the-air activities started in grade school. Every year I saved my allowance to spend on rides at the carnival when it came to town during Apple Blossom time. The excitement of spinning, twisting and being upside down still sends shivers up my spine. As soon as the rides were functional and ready, I was there, even if it was a school night.

Over the years, I searched for more adventure. Parasailing behind a motorboat on Lake Chelan was new when I graduated from high school. As I approached the watchful eyes of the people in charge, I knew I needed to convince them, "I really can do this." I don't believe they ever had an amputee sail behind one of their boats before. The challenge was doing a land start which took a couple of steps before lift-off. I had no doubt I would be up in the air in no time, but I can understand their apprehension. With a cute guy on each side holding my arms for balance, two hops and I was in the air. Looking down into the clear

Skiing Uphill

Pat parasailing in Mazatlan

water of the lake, I saw old pilings of docks that were no longer floating on top. Years later, I parasailed in Mazatlán, Mexico. The reason I did it a second time was the line was longer, and once again, I had two cute guys by my side for support.

Zip-lining caught my eye while searching for activities to do in Mazatlán, Mexico. What a rush, skimming over the tops of the trees, suspended by a thin cable. At the second landing, I noticed the rigging was secured together with both electrician and duct tape. No OSHA rules there. I was the first amputee not wearing a prosthesis to zip with this company. Again, I posed new challenges for the guys. The young men kept me safe to zip again. One even gave me a piggyback ride up the steep hill when I started getting overheated.

Next came my birthday surprise from Joe. He had booked an appointment for me to go up in a glider with a pilot out of the Pangborn Memorial Airport in East Wenatchee. Over the years, I watched gliders from afar. Now, it was my turn to fly with the birds.

It became spooky quiet after the motored plane flew to a safe elevation, released the tow cable, and set us free to ride the wind currents. Quickly, the pilot realized I was

Pat and Glider Pilot, Pangborn Airport

enjoying the experience and wasn't going to get sick. Only then did we do some dives and twists, reminding me of my carnival riding days.

When a neighbor moved across the street from our home, I had the opportunity to ride in a small, sport plane for two. He built the LongEZE aircraft from a kit. What a thrill it was for me to fly over the Enchantments, a popular hiking area outside of Leavenworth. Since I don't hike, I would never have seen the beauty of these mountains and lakes without this adventure. For a bonus, I snapped the perfect picture of Mt. Rainer against a bluebird sky.

Each up-in-the-air activity added a different excitement. In the summer of 2017, I topped them all. During a contest at WORX gym, I won a tandem skydive with Dive Chelan. My gym friends asked if I was

*Pat with LongEZE, a plane built
from a kit by a neighbor*

really going to dive. "Yes, or I wouldn't have placed the tickets I got during the contest in the skydive jar." The look on the presenter's face after he drew my name and I rolled up in my wheelchair was priceless.

Sitting on the edge to exit the plane,

Skiing Uphill

11,000 feet above the ground, truly took my breath away. Did I think about backing out? Never!!! We inched toward the edge... one more skooch... and we were in a 100-mile-an-hour free fall dive! My only regret was that everything happened so fast. Would I do it again? In a heartbeat!!!

Ryan, the man I dove with, was a child I had watched grow up when racing on our ski hill. He was a cute kid who turned into a handsome man. I didn't mind being tethered to him while experiencing the thrill of my life.

My last up-in-the-air adventure was when Joe and I rode in a hot air balloon in

Skydiving with Dive Chelan with Ryan

October of 2017. It was so quiet until the burners turned on to lift us higher. Floating over the fields and surveying the incredible landscape gave a unique perspective of the many colors and textures below us. I became concerned when I saw the landing area coming, a potato field with mounded rows, not exactly flat. The pilot gently sat us down, the basket did tip on its side, but that made it easier to get out instead of up over the edge.

And, of course, I must mention the incredible helicopter tour that Joe and I took over the island of Kauai, Hawaii. The beauty from up there was magnificent.

One more up-in-the-air item on my bucket list used to be to jump off the cliff at Chelan Butte and tandem hang glide. This poses different challenges, and I haven't

Helicopter tour of Kauai, Hawaii

been cleared to schedule this adventure. I can wait as safety comes first. I know the experience is still there waiting. But the longer I wait it's not as appealing as it once was. For now, I'll pass and view the pictures reliving all the adventures of the past.

Gym Rat

Chapter 18

The importance of moving and strengthening muscles became more evident after visiting a friend in an assisted living facility. What I observed made it clear if I don't take my health and physical shape seriously, I won't be able to do what I want to do. I understand all the residents are several years older than me, and I don't know what their lives were like in their younger days. Even now, I know when I don't move, I want to move less. When I move less, I get stiff and gain weight. This visual at the facility helped me make the choice not to enter my golden years overweight and under-exercised. That is when I became a gym rat.

I have been active most of my life, as I have described in the previous chapters, such as skiing in the winter, biking in the spring and summer, and now bowling. When I was teaching, I didn't have the energy to work out at the gym after a full day at school during the week.

After retirement, everything changed. I

was beginning to think that retirement was highly overrated. Something was missing. Then I realized what it was, I needed more interaction with people. I'm not sure why I decided to check out a couple of gyms. I guess because I knew there were people there. After visiting two local gyms, I knew the one I didn't want to go to. On entering the first facility, I asked the girl at the desk if there were classes to observe to see if that was something I could do. A yoga class was about to start and that sounded like something I might like. I already had workout clothes on and wanted to try the class. I walked in the door and before introductions were made or anything else was said, the instructor sighed and said, "Well, I have to change what I had planned today! That immediately got me fired up, "NO, you don't, I'm here to see if I can do this or not." I stayed the hour but never went back.

The second gym was different. One of the trainers had time to talk with me about her class of kinesis. I told her I was there checking out if this was something I was able to do. Before we started, she asked if I was nervous "a little," I said "Are you? "A little," she answered. I had a good feeling from the start and took her class for seven years until the gym changed its emphasis, which didn't include that class. In those seven years, I officially became a gym rat with a new family of like-minded friends. Feeling emotionally, mentally, and physically stronger over the ten years, I'm always looking for other exercise opportunities to keep me motivated. Along with the class, I also expanded my workout to include weights, rowing, and hand cycle machines and a diverse number of resistant machines. The family of gym rats has grown, and I'm accountable to them when not there, so there is built-in accountability. It's also a positive place to be.

A week after I joined this gym, I went to a yoga class in the afternoon to see if this was something I could do. The third week I attended I was between two twenty-something girls who were fit and limber. As we went through the poses, I became more and more aware of my age and ability, sixty-something. My emotions started creeping to the surface as time went on, but I held them in check and left the gym, talking to no one nor looking left or right. Reaching the safety of my car I broke down into gasping, breathless sobs. When I calmed down and felt it was safe, I drove home. Upon arriving, I decided to water the plants on our deck. Joe came home shortly thereafter and parked in his garage. As he was walking by the deck, he asked, "How was the class?" Once again, I broke down into sobbing cries. He jumped onto the deck and wanted to know what happened. Looking him straight in the eye with a scrunched-up face, I said, "It's not fair, I want my leg, and I want it now," while poking my finger into his thigh. He held me and I calmed down until I looked into his eyes again. Then, I started gasping the same cry while expressing the same demand, "I want my leg back, and I want it NOW!" He held me until the sobs abated. I was exhausted and told him I was okay and as soon as I finished watering the plants, I would come into the house.

What made the cleansing of emotions okay? I was getting a drink of water at the kitchen sink that night, when he came up behind me, wrapped his arms around me, and simply said, "Pat if you hadn't lost your leg, we would have never met." That's proof something good comes out of every experience.

The yoga teacher assured me that my reaction was a normal reaction to participating in yoga classes because yoga opens avenues for the trauma of the past to be released. Boy, were they released!

I brought new challenges for all the trainers to adapt activities for me to be able to do without my crutches, and now from a wheelchair. Never have the staff treated me like they aren't interested in helping me like in that first gym. It's no surprise the first gym isn't in business anymore.

Anywhere I go, there is a possibility of a mishap, and the gym turned out to be no different. I attended the cycling class for years, until recently. Even with the issue of sitting on the narrow seat, I had been on and off the bike hundreds of times. One day I slipped off the side of the seat getting on and crashed to the floor. I hit the metal mount on the floor with the back of my head and ended up with ten staples. As Sue Northey said:" Scars are a roadmap of my life." My body looks like I've been around the world a few times.

Using only one leg for years makes it even more important to protect my knee and hip, especially because my hip was dislocated in the car accident. The way to do this is by keeping the surrounding muscles strong. Working out at the gym regularly has not kept away all the aches, spasms, and occasional numbness, but has made me stronger. I'm also mindful of how

I move so as not to twist my knee. Again, muscle strength is necessary.

Balance is more of an issue as I've gotten older. Now I must swallow my pride and use a wheelchair at the gym. It was either that or stop going and I knew that was not an option. I don't want to think about where I would be physically if I had not developed the habit of exercise.

Besides my fitness and safety, it is another way to encourage people. They see my determination to do what is necessary to stay strong by using what I have, and not making excuses. I am motivated even more when members approach me and acknowledge my persistence. That, in turn, encourages me to continue.

Even at the gym, challenges are many, but then that's what my life is about, adapting. So far, I've refused to let challenges stop me.

Everything we find time to do is a choice, whether it's productive or not. I know since I have set aside a specific time at the gym, I am stronger, happier, and have more energy to do what needs to be done with the rest of my day. If you have never managed to find the time to work out, give yourself a head start heading toward your Golden Years and start today. It's not too late. We all have

Skiing Uphill

Pat at the gym

challenges and need to push through them by doing what we can. In what direction will you take your first step to a healthier life? Come on, join a family of gym rats.

Who Knew? I am Creative!

Chapter 19

For decades, I carried around the belief that I was NOT creative. False as it has turned out to be, that was my truth since one of my elementary teachers threw my picture into the garbage. I was raised on a farm and had many fun things to do outside like ride the calf, chase chickens, ride bikes, or climb around in the hay loft. During those times, I didn't give school experience a second thought. But back in class when art time came around and it was time to put something down on that big white sheet of paper, I got nervous. I also had to prepare myself for the possibility that it might end up in the garbage again. I eventually complied with the assignment but not before looking around to get ideas from more creative classmates.

I learned years later that I wasn't the only child who experienced this feeling of artistic isolation in elementary school, of all places. A friend told me about a study conducted with kindergarten and third-grade students. Both groups were instructed, "Raise your hand if you are an artist"? One hundred percent of the kindergarteners raised their hands. The same question was asked of the third graders and a mere ten percent raised their hands. This was a good life lesson to remember when I became a schoolteacher.

Slowly, I found creative outlets in my adult years through crocheting, watercolor painting as well as painting kindness rocks, and writing. Unfortunately, the latter three activities didn't happen until after I retired from teaching. If I could have a 'do over,' this is something I would like to change. I was a compliant girl most of my life so it's hard to do anything without thinking about whether I am doing it right or doing it wrong. I have learned that it is not healthy to think that way, because it is never productive or doesn't get you anywhere. Now I enjoy sharing my crafts with people and I don't worry about how they might "grade" me or what they might do with my gift.

When was the last time a stranger came up to you and gave something that brought an instant smile to your face AND was useful? That's the fun I have with my bookworms. Recently, we spent three weeks on the island of Kauai. I took three hundred of my hand-crocheted bookworm bookmarkers. I had taken two for my books but left them as well. On every vacation, I take a hundred for each week we are there. It's amazing the friendships that have developed through these crazy little creatures, plus they are enjoyable conversation starters.

I also joined a knitting group of very accomplished women. Often, I was the entertainment because my stitches kept going in all directions except the right way. After weeks of patient instructions and laughter, I eventually mastered a style of scarf, and then I was promoted to nesting bowls. Both were great Christmas gifts for neighbors and friends, especially when the bowls were filled with candy.

Since I was comfortable with those two activities, it was time to add something new. When I first tried my hand at painting, that familiar feeling of inferiority popped up as I realized that everything, I had previously created, was created from a pattern. I was in a box with extremely high sides of "right and wrong," called instructions. My new challenge was to get OUT of that box. Like anything new, it has been, and sometimes still is, painful but the rewards and encouragement from my husband and friends keep me going.

Skiing Uphill

I started taking classes in watercolor painting. Remembering that teacher who threw my painting in the trash can in elementary school gave me the desire to prove that I am creative. The first painting teacher I had asked all in attendance why they were there. After I told her about my experience, she came to my table, enveloped both hands, and said, "You are safe here."

This is where I met my friend, author, artist, and international speaker, Judi Moreo. Again, another connection was made through sharing bookworms. After the painting class, we met for an extended lunch and started sharing our stories. She encouraged me to write articles for her magazine even though I had never written so much as a poem in my life. Starting with short articles, I became more confident with the thought of writing a book. She saw a story that needed to be told and through her faith, my story is being shared.

My newest artistic venture is inspirational, also called "kindness rock" painting. There is freedom in painting with acrylics. If I don't like the finished product, I give it a new base coat and start over.

Once again, I'm in my comfort zone using a pattern. Pinterest is my new favorite place to visit. Through social media, I get hundreds of ideas daily. My painting of the quotes and silly creatures brings a smile to the faces of those who see them. The only rule I follow: If I don't smile at the picture, I don't paint it. Examples of phrases I use are I Lava You; Don't Go Bacon My Heart; You're One in a Melon; Orange You Glad We Met; and Dill with It. From there the list is endless. More thoughtful sayings: Yesterday was heavy, put it down; A mistake is a bruise, not a tattoo; When your world gets rocky, rock your world: Nothing is written in stone; Every storm runs out of rain, and I have more ideas to come, I'm sure.

I tease sometimes with my rocks, too. I painted rocks for two college roommates that said "Friends" at the top. Then I painted three silly, fuzzy faces on stick figures. One of the figures only had one leg. I waited to see how long it took them to notice. I painted two ladybugs holding hands. My husband said he wanted one. I handed him one that I had already painted, and he said, "No," I want one with one leg." "Oh, Joe."

Artist, author, adventurer, all despite being an amputee. Who would have believed I could do all these things? Yet, I can and so can you. I appreciate everyone who has encouraged and discouraged me along the way. Every experience made me who I am today and strengthened my resolve to be the strongest person, both physically and mentally that I can be. The life lesson I have learned is, "The only thing I can do wrong is NOT do anything." I am holding on to that truth and wondering, "Hum-m-m... what's next?"

"Through the eyes of gratitude, everything is a miracle."

Mary Davis

Author, Everyday Spirit

AFTERWORD

I am blessed to have taught children for thirty-eight years in two states and three different schools, covering grades from kindergarten through Middle School as well as being a substitute teacher in all disciplines in elementary schools, fourteen of the thirty-eight years. Twenty-four of these years were spent working with learning disabled children. Showing up for each new challenge sends a message to people that despite what happens to us, we can go on, and live meaningful lives. Every ending makes room for a new beginning.

I have tried to set a good example all my years. I believe, through it all, I have proven more than once that it is possible to ski up the hill of life and win.

HOMETOWN HERO

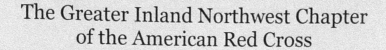

The Greater Inland Northwest Chapter
of the American Red Cross

is honored to recognize

Pat Turner

2019 Hometown Heroes Nominee

*In celebration of your heroism and service
to the communities of North Central Washington*

Megan Snow
Executive Director

Doug Jones
Board of Directors

American Red Cross

I am nominating Pat Turner for the Hometown Hero Award for two main reasons, but she deserves it for many more. I moved to Wenatchee less than three years ago and have only known Pat for a little over a year. There are people in Entiat (where Pat grew up) and Wenatchee (where she has lived most of her adult life) who could write much more in-depth about why she deserves this award than I can, but she has inspired me so much in this past year that I simply am compelled to nominate her.

Pat has done an incredible amount of volunteering over the years, but my acquaintance with her comes through the writing group that she established a couple of years ago, which meets weekly at Pybus Market. She facilitates the group which is open to anyone who wants to come, and there is no charge. She describes the purpose of the group as "writing for clarity." All of us in the group have improved in our ability to articulate our thoughts in writing and in our willingness to share them. Pat is always there early with everything ready for us including inspirational quotes, constructive writing pointers from various sources, and best of all, the most welcoming smile for all the regulars, guests, and newcomers. Many of us have become motivated to work on writing our memoirs because of Pat.

I have been talking to my daughter in Florida for a year about how great this group is and about Pat, but it turns out I had never mentioned to her that Pat is missing her right leg.

In a recent conversation, I mentioned it casually as I was talking to her about the group. My daughter was totally surprised! I say this because it reveals that her disability does not define who she is or what she can do. She lost her leg in a car accident when she was in high school. Her story is traumatic and heartbreaking. Her determination to live the fullest possible life despite this loss has taken her from the ski slopes to skydiving and most everything in between. She wrote a great article about these pursuits in The Good Life magazine this past fall. Pat and her husband, Joe, can often be seen riding their tandem bike on the Apple Loop Trail.

Her positivity, openness, honesty, generosity, friendliness, and empathy are a few of the virtues that define her. She is widely known in the community as a person you absolutely need to get to know! She is and has been a role model in the Wenatchee Valley and beyond for over 50 years, especially for anyone who struggles with physical challenges.

I am blessed to call her my friend and for me, she is one of the most heroic people I have ever known.

Linda Reid

CPSIA information can be obtained
at www.ICGtesting.com
Printed in the USA
BVHW061954070123
655676BV00003B/9

9 780996 881746